KINSHIP AND MARRIAGE
AMONG THE NUER

A wedding dance

KINSHIP AND MARRIAGE
AMONG THE NUER

BY

E. E. EVANS-PRITCHARD

PROFESSOR OF SOCIAL ANTHROPOLOGY
AND FELLOW OF ALL SOULS COLLEGE
IN THE UNIVERSITY OF OXFORD

OXFORD
AT THE CLARENDON PRESS

Oxford University Press, Ely House, London W. 1

GLASGOW NEW YORK TORONTO MELBOURNE WELLINGTON
CAPE TOWN SALISBURY IBADAN NAIROBI LUSAKA ADDIS ABABA
BOMBAY CALCUTTA MADRAS KARACHI LAHORE DACCA
KUALA LUMPUR SINGAPORE HONG KONG TOKYO

FIRST PUBLISHED 1951
REPRINTED LITHOGRAPHICALLY IN GREAT BRITAIN
AT THE UNIVERSITY PRESS, OXFORD
BY VIVIAN RIDLER, PRINTER TO THE UNIVERSITY
FROM SHEETS OF THE FIRST EDITION
1961, 1965, 1966, 1969

PREFACE

In 1940 I published under the title *The Nuer: A Description of the Modes of Livelihood and Political Institutions of a Nilotic People,* referred to henceforward as *The Nuer,* the first part of a general summary of the information collected during twelve months spent among the Nuer of the Nilotic Sudan in the years 1930, 1931, 1935, and 1936. The present volume forms the second part of this general account. I had planned to publish it in 1942 and it was already partly written before the war. During the years of war military service compelled me to relinquish literary work, and the completion of the book has since been further delayed by academic duties and also by a change of interests which led me to give my first attention to a history of the Sanusi of Cyrenaica.

The Nuer are a Nilotic people of between 200,000 and 300,000 souls living in savannah country near the Upper Nile and its tributaries. They are a cattle people, the ebb and flow of whose transhumant life follow the seasons. They are divided into a number of tribes, the largest political groups of their society, and these tribes are segmented into sections and subsections corresponding structurally to the segments, or lineages, of the clans dominant in each tribal territory. In *The Nuer* I described the form of segmentation in political and descent groups and I attempted to show the principles which underlie it. I also gave a short account of the age-set system; but I omitted all but the briefest references to marriage, family, and kinship because I believe that political structure presents problems which are better inquired into apart from social relations of a different kind.

In this second volume I first show that the members of a Nuer village or camp are not only kith but also kin, and how the network of kinship ties within local communities is connected with the lineage system of the Nuer and through that system with their tribal, or political, constitution. This demonstration serves as a bridge between the theme of my earlier book and the subject of marriage to which the present volume is largely devoted. The network of kinship ties within any Nuer community can ultimately be reduced to a series of marriage unions. Among the Nuer, as in all human societies, marriage and the family are the most fundamental institutions.

The role of kinship values in Nuer society cannot be understood

(v)

PREFACE
unless the range of prohibited degrees in marriage is taken into account. For this reason, and also because it would seem the logical order of treating the various topics relating to marriage, I discuss marriage prohibitions and incest before describing in Chapter III the steps by which marriage is brought about—courtship, ceremonies, payment of bridewealth, birth of a firstborn, and the observance of formal rules of behaviour between affinal relatives —and the various forms of marriage and concubinage found among the Nuer.

I discuss in the two final chapters some features of the family, the group brought into existence by marriage, and kinship, the system of categories of relationship which derives from the family. I have not been able to treat these two topics as exhaustively as their importance demands. A second year among the Nuer would have been necessary to cover them satisfactorily.

I have given in *The Nuer* a full bibliography up to the year 1939. Since then various articles have been published by others* and by myself,† and a dictionary of the Nuer language has appeared.‡

I make acknowledgement for the use I have made of my own articles to the Editors of *Sudan Notes and Records, Uganda Journal, Africa, African Studies, Zeitschrift für Vergleichende Rechtswissenschaft, Social Structure, African Systems of Kinship and Marriage*, and *Man*, and to the Director of the Rhodes–Livingstone Institute. Much detail omitted in this book is recorded in these articles.

* A. H. Alban, 'Gwek's Pipe and Pyramid', *S.N. & R.*, 1940; P. Coriat, 'Gwek, the Witch-Doctor and the Pyramid of Dengkur', ibid. 1939; P. P. Howell, 'A Note on Elephants and Elephant Hunting among the Nuer', ibid. 1945; 'On the Value of Iron among the Nuer', *Man*, 1947; (with B. A. Lewis) 'Nuer Ghouls: a Form of Witchcraft', *S.N. & R.*, 1947; 'The Age-Set System and the Institution of *"Nak"* among the Nuer', ibid. 1948; F. D. Kingdon, 'The Western Nuer Patrol 1927–8', ibid. 1945.

† 'The Nuer of the Southern Sudan', *African Political Systems*, 1940; 'Nuer Bridewealth', *Africa*, 1946; 'Bridewealth among the Nuer', *African Studies*, 1947; 'Nuer Marriage Ceremonies', *Africa*, 1947; 'A Note on Courtship among the Nuer', *S.N. & R.*, 1947; 'A Note on Affinity Relationships among the Nuer', *Man*, 1948; 'Nuer Modes of Address', *Uganda Journal*, 1948; 'The Nuer *Col Wic*', *Man*, 1949; 'Burial and Mortuary Rites of the Nuer', *African Affairs*, 1949; 'Nuer Rules of Exogamy and Incest', *Social Structure*, 1949; 'Two Nuer Ritual Concepts', *Man*, 1949; 'Nuer Totemism', *Annali Lateranensi*, 1949; 'Nuer Curses and Ghostly Vengeance', *Africa*, 1949; 'The Nuer Family', *S.N. & R.*, 1950.

‡ Father J. Kiggen, *Nuer–English Dictionary*, 1948 (based on the manuscripts of Father J. P. Crazzolara).

My study of the Nuer was made on behalf of the Government of the Anglo-Egyptian Sudan, to whom I am again indebted for financial assistance towards costs of publication. In *The Nuer* I have already thanked those friends, missionaries and administrative officers, who helped me in the Sudan. I express to the following gentlemen my appreciation of their kindness in reading the manuscript of this book: Dr. M. N. Srinivas, Mr. R. G. Lienhardt, and Mr. K. O. L. Burridge.

I dedicate it to my friend and teacher, Professor A. R. Radcliffe-Brown, whose vast knowledge and illuminating analyses of primitive kinship systems have placed all students of the subject in his debt.

E. E. E-P.

OXFORD
July 1950

CONTENTS

LIST OF PLATES

MAPS AND FIGURES

*The last two illustrations are from drawings of
specimens collected by the author
and now in the Museum of
Archaeology and Ethnology,
Cambridge.*

CHAPTER I

KINSHIP AND THE LOCAL COMMUNITY

I

In *The Nuer* I stated that the village is the smallest corporate group of a political kind among the Nuer and that in reading my description of their political structure the reader would have to take for granted the network of kinship and affinal ties within a village. I must now ask him to remember that, though I describe in this book relationships between persons within local communities without again describing the wider political structure, the local communities within which these relationships function and which they serve to maintain are the basic units of that structure. I must also make it plain that in *The Nuer* I was chiefly interested in the relation of clan segmentation to tribal segmentation, and therefore in discussing lineages gave chief attention to the systematic form their structure presents when co-ordinated with tribal, or political, structure. To avoid misunderstanding it is desirable to emphasize that in Nuerland there are also small lineages which have fewer branches and less depth than the dominant clans to which I gave particular attention in my book. These less systematized descent groups may be associated with local communities smaller than tribes and their larger segments, but they are only associated with them in terms of the tribal structure as a whole through some relationship to its dominant clan; and sometimes they are not associated with local communities at all.

The Nuer village (*cieng*) is a corporate group with a feeling of solidarity. Though its members have contacts with persons in neighbouring villages, and even in other sections of their tribe and in adjacent tribes, the greater part of their activities are carried out within their own village community and their strongest ties are generally with other members of it. Nuer have great affection for their homes and, in spite of their wandering habits, men born and bred in a village are likely to return to it even if they live elsewhere for some years. Villagers fight side by side in defence and attack and they support one another in feuds. When their youths attend dances in the district they enter them in a war line (*dep*) singing their special war chant, and they remain together during the dancing lest some incident should lead to fighting, for it sometimes happens that when the dancing parties of different villages duel their play passes into fighting. Villagers also have close economic relations and common economic interests which make a village a corporation owning its cultivations, water-supplies, fishing-pools, and grazing grounds; the ownership being spoken about in terms of the lineage with which the village is socially identified. There is, especially in the smaller villages, much co-operation in labour and much sharing of food. At the beginning of the drought the villagers may scatter to camp round different pools in the bush and some families, and even large aggregates of relatives, may spend the dry season with kinsmen of different villages, but the scattering is temporary. As a rule, families which live in the same village in the rains share the same cattle camp (*wec*) at the height of the drought.

Nevertheless, in spite of their many contacts with one another and of their concerted action in their relations with other villages, there may be rivalries between members of different parts of a single village. This is more noticeable in the larger villages, where groups of kin occupy distinct sections of the village site and have a feeling of exclusiveness towards each other. '*Wa pekda*', 'I go to my end (of the village)', often indicates, besides direction, a sectional loyalty.

Nuer villages, called after the names of their sites, vary in size and form, both of which depend largely on local conditions. Some are small communities of not more than a few families living on riverside mounds, accumulations of debris which have been dwelling places for long periods. They may be regarded as colonies attached to larger communities. Larger villages, of some hundreds of souls, are generally strung out along the backs of ridges, but where there is a wide stretch of high ground a village may be distributed in all directions over several miles of country.

Indeed, it is a characteristic of all Nuer villages, to which Jules Poncet alludes,* that they are spread out as freely as the nature of the ground permits in little groups of habitations, each separated generally from its neighbours by some fifty to several hundred paces. A group of this kind often consists of a single homestead, a cattle byre with its attendant hut or huts, the dwelling of a family.

* Jules Poncet, *Le Fleuve Blanc*, 1863–4, p. 40.

The Nuer speak of a man's homestead as his *gol*, the primary meaning of which word is the heap of smouldering cattle-dung in the centre of a byre and the hearth around it. In its narrowest social use the word means family, the occupants of the homestead, and it may also therefore have the further sense of household, since there may be other persons living there than members of the owner's family who count nevertheless, as we would say, as members of the family. Frequently the byres and huts of two or three families, the heads of which are commonly brothers or a man and his married sons, are grouped around a common kraal so that we may then speak of a composite homestead; or several homesteads, owned generally by close kin, are adjacent to one another and form distinct clusters which we may call hamlets. Nuer speak of a composite homestead as the *gol* of so-and-so, naming its senior member, although they also refer to each of its component homesteads as the *gol* of its particular owner. They may use the same word to describe what I have called a hamlet, though a cluster of this kind with the land around it is also designated by the word *dhor*, combined with the name either of its senior member, as *dhor* Nyang, the hamlet of Nyang, or of some natural feature, as *dhor ngop*, the hamlet of the wild fig-tree. In its widest connotation *gol* may have the sense of 'lineage', when a lineage is thought of as a residential group. The word *cieng*, which has the general sense of 'home', may be employed to describe a residential group of any size, from single homestead to large tribal division. It is usually coupled with the name of a lineage when it refers to local groups of any size.

When Nuer leave their villages in the dry season they collect, often after temporary dispersal, in large waterside camps. There is then greater solidarity, both spatial and moral, than in the rains. The community of a camp is crowded together in grass windscreens and little grass beehive huts, and the herds which in the rains are tethered in separate kraals are now tethered in the same kraal or in adjacent kraals. In the rains, when water is abundant and pasturage near at hand, the cattle are either not herded at all or each family, or a group of adjacent families, herds its own; but in the dry season, when conditions are different, the cattle of a camp are watered and pastured together and the different families take it in turn to provide herdsmen. Activities performed of necessity or by preference in parties—hunting, fishing, and collecting—

cooperation in work in dry season

are dry-season activities. Also, milking, cleaning kraals, making up fires, cooking, pounding grain, and other chores which are performed separately and at different times by each household in the villages tend to be performed in unison in the camps. The greater density of the community and the rigours of the season impose a common regimen. Another feature of cattle camps which has some social importance is their composition. Neighbouring village communities which in the rains occupy different sites, often divided by wide swamps, frequently make common camp or they camp so near to each other that there are more intimate relations between their members in the dry season. The radius of effective kinship is greater in the dry season than in the wet.

Although there is this greater cohesion in camps, the families and joint families and larger clusters of kin whose social distinction is evident in the distribution of homesteads in the villages maintain their identity in the distribution of camp windscreens and huts. Each family has its own windscreen, corresponding to its byre in the village, and in the centre of it is the *gol*, its hearth of ashes. Attached to the windscreen are the beehive huts of the womenfolk, just as in the villages their wattle-and-daub huts are attached to the byre. The windscreens of those whose homesteads adjoin in the villages are generally adjacent to, almost touching, one another in the camps and form clearly demarcated rows in the circle of camp dwellings. When a large village is clearly segmented, the separation observable in the distribution of its homesteads can also be noted in the dispersal of smaller camps within the general camping area. These social alinements are most evident in the early part of the dry season, before the large concentrations of the main season have been formed, for then small groups of kin often make independent camps around isolated pools at some, sometimes a considerable, distance from each other.

II

All the members of such a village or camp as I have briefly described are kin. Before giving examples in illustration of this statement I must say again what I have already said in *The Nuer* about the difference between lineage relations and kin relations because it is a very important difference. In speaking of lineages I refer to unilateral groups of kin—among the Nuer groups of agnates—and in speaking of kinship I refer to categories of kin. In speaking of lineage relations I therefore refer to relations between groups within a system of such groups, whereas in speaking of kin, or kinship, relations I refer to relations between persons standing to one another in certain categories of relationship within a system of such categories. It is often difficult for those who have not lived in a society with a lineage structure to appreciate the distinction I have drawn because the relationship between collateral lineages of the same clan is necessarily also one that can be expressed in terms of a kinship category, and it is possible in certain circumstances even to speak of the relation between lineages of different clans in similar terms, for they may wish on occasions to stress a genealogical nexus between themselves, indicating thereby that, for example, the one stand to the other as *gaatnar*, children of the maternal uncle, or as *gaatwac*, children of the paternal aunt. But in these cases it is a relationship between groups that is referred to and not a personal relationship between individuals except in so far as it is derived from the relationship between the groups to which they belong.

As I have explained in *The Nuer*, the lineages of Nuerland are dispersed groups, though in a certain sense they may be regarded as corporate groups in the form they take as political segments in fusion with other elements. They provide the conceptual framework of the political system within which they also function as its organizing principle through the expression of political fission and fusion in terms of their segmentary structure. The identification of lineage segments with tribal segments in a political context is brought about by the acknowledgement that certain clans and their lineages have rights in certain tribal areas and by the residence in those areas of a sufficient number of members of these dominant groups to act as nuclei of local and political groups. It probably never happens that all members of a lineage of any order—maximal, major, minor, or minimal—live in the area associated with it and to which it gives its name, though very many of them may do so.

Because the usual reference to a lineage is in a political context it is generally spoken of as the *cieng* of such-and-such a people (the name of the lineage being given), for, like the word *gol*, *cieng* has always a residential, and not an exclusive descent, connotation. When reference is made to a lineage in a context in which it is desired to particularize it as an exclusive descent group, a group of agnatic kin descended from a common ancestor, Nuer use the expressions *thok dwiel* or *thok mac*, literally the doorway to a hut or the hearth, to denote it; but these expressions are little used because abstraction of a lineage from its social and political matrix has only rarely to be made: on certain ritual occasions and in connexion with feuds and rules of exogamy.

The distinction between an agnatic lineage relation and an agnatic kinship relation is clearly made by Nuer themselves, from whom indeed I learnt it. They use the word *buth* to describe agnatic kinship between collateral lineages, that is to say, kinship between groups and between individuals only in virtue of their membership of these groups. On the other hand, they use the word *mar* to describe any and every relationship of a kinship kind between persons. All persons with whom a man acknowledges any kind of kinship, through however many other persons, are *mar*, kin, to him. People say of him and of any such person '*teke mar*', 'they have kinship'; and he speaks of any or all of his relations as '*jimarida*', 'my kinsmen'. The term *mar* includes relatives through the mother, the maternal kin, and through the father, the paternal kin. This is the meaning the word has when used by Nuer collectively and without restrictive qualification. Its sphere of reference is indicative of the balance we find in social life generally between the paternal kin and the maternal kin, a balance evident in the configurations of kin in local communities which I am about to describe. Nuer also sometimes use *mar* when speaking of affinal relations, especially when they are long established. In a broad sense they also are kin in the eyes of Nuer, just as in our own society we include our affines in the category of relatives.

Where there is a *buth* relationship between lineages there must also, in one way of speaking, be *mar* between the members of one and the members of the other, for the relationship between collateral lineages is agnatic and the members of the one must therefore be patrilineal kin to the members of the other. The question therefore arises: at what point in the spread of an agnatic line, conceived of as a number of living patrilineal kinsmen, does interpersonal *mar* relationship become the inter-group relationship Nuer call *buth* so that these kinsmen divide into segmentary descent groups or lineages? The question may be put in another way: how many generations back do Nuer trace patrilineal ascent

(6)

before they reach the first ancestor from whom bifurcate collateral lines of descent of the kind they call a *thok dwiel*, a lineage?

A Nuer, when asked about this matter, gave an historical explanation: 'In the days when people scattered, brother and son went raiding and they settled where they raided. Then kinship ceased (*ce mar thuk*) and there remained only a lineage relationship (*ce dwoth ni buth*).' This could only have happened, however, as Nuer themselves say, after some generations had elapsed. Even today descendants of Nuer who settled to the east of the Nile, after raiding the Dinka in what are now the Jikany and Lou tribal areas, sometimes travel to the homes of their forebears to the west of the Nile to receive cattle which are their due on the marriages of the daughters of kinsmen from whose fathers and grandfathers their fathers and grandfathers separated. While the privileges of kinship are thus claimed, the persons concerned cannot be regarded as *jibuthni*, members of collateral lineages. Indeed, in my experience, Nuer do not generally speak of lineages till four or five generations back in patrilineal ascent, and I think also that there are good technical reasons for following Nuer usage in this matter and for not speaking of lineages before at least the third generation is reached.

Although any relative of a man is *mar* to him, the word most frequently refers to close relatives only, and on the paternal side generally implies those persons on the marriage of whose daughters a man can claim a portion of the bridewealth proper, which means an agnatic relationship deriving from any forebear as far back as, but not beyond, the bride's great grandfather. Nuer commonly explain such matters in terms of cattle-rights. Also it is for descendants of the great grandfather that specific kinship terms are used in their primary reference. It is this grouping, in relation to any person, of agnates of three generations in depth that I shall have in mind when I speak of a man's paternal kin.

Beyond this point we enter into the structural relations of the lineage system where the Nuer begin to speak of collectivities of agnates. There is always *buth* between collateral lineages of the same clan and there may also be *buth* between clans, as I have explained in *The Nuer*. Also, a captured Dinka boy may be *lath buthni*, given *buth*, and thereby made a member of his captor's lineage. Groups which have no *buth* have *rul* between them, that is, they are 'strangers'. I omit further discussion about the inter-relations of collateral lineages because they do not here directly concern us.

<h2 style="text-align:center">III</h2>

Having made what preliminary explanations seemed to be necessary, I record some examples of the network of kinship ties in typical Nuer villages and camps.

As I have said earlier, members of a village are all *mar*, kin, to one another: any villager can trace kinship to every other person in his village, either by a direct kinship tie or through a third person who is in different ways related both to himself and the other person. Furthermore, he can establish kinship of some kind —real, by analogy, mythological, or assumed—with everybody he comes into contact with during his lifetime and throughout the length and breadth of Nuerland; and this is necessary if he has frequent dealings with them, for all social obligation of a personal kind is defined in terms of kinship. But within his local community the links are definite and well known. All members of a village or cattle camp can be placed on a single genealogical chart showing relationship by blood, adoption, and marriage.

The village of Konye is on a site on the left bank of the Pibor and a few miles to the south of Akobo Post. It is on the periphery of Nuerland, on their present-day frontier with the Anuak, and has only recently been used by Nuer, of the Lou tribe, as a permanent wet-season settlement, though they have probably long camped on the site in seasons of severe drought. Nevertheless, the social cluster found in occupation of it in May 1935 is typical of small communities in every part of Nuerland. In that year the village consisted of eleven homesteads perched on a high mound some eighty paces in diameter with four attached homesteads lying between four hundred and six hundred paces to the south of the mound. On a rough estimate the population of the village and attached homesteads was eighty to a hundred souls. I spent only a few days in the village and restricted my inquiries there to an effort to discover its genealogical pattern by ascertaining the kinship ties between the men who owned the fifteen cattle byres, that is to say, between the fifteen heads of families of the settlement. This might seem a simple task, but in Nuerland, where people do not co-operate in an inquiry of this kind, it is by no means so, and the genealogy had to be pieced together by asking why each owner of a byre had come to live at Konye, a question answered by mentioning his relationship to someone already living in the village. There may be other ties of kinship or affinity between members of the different families which have not been recorded. There may also be more domestic unions other than the union of simple legal marriage than those shown on the chart. Irregular unions are not easily unearthed in a rapid survey which is not directed to that end. The genealogical table, which includes the owners of the outlying homesteads, is not a complete record of all the persons living at Konye.

The chief man of the village is Rue-Wor (homestead 8), and his son Deng-Rue (homestead 12) is the chief man of the outlying hamlet. The community is grouped round Rue, who, although he belongs to the Gaawar clan and therefore counts as a stranger (*rul*) and not as an aristocrat (*dil*) in the Lou tribal territory where he resides, is the *tut*, the 'bull', as Nuer say, of this community. A man holding this social position is also sometimes referred to as *ruei wec*, an expression which appears to mean 'spittle of the camp (community)'. There are several Lou tribal aristocrats in the village, but they have only a lineage, and no special personal status in it. Kinsmen of the villagers from the interior of Lou country spend the dry season in the village.

I direct attention to some features of the genealogy which are typical of many small Nuer communities. The Konye community is not in itself in any sense a lineage group, though it is attached politically to one of the dominant Jinaca lineages of the Lou tribe. Its nucleus is the family of Rue-Wor, the 'bull' of the village, and linked to it, some in one way and some in another, are a group of kin related to Rue and to each other. Any relationship of a man with any other member of the community serves to attach him to it and to give him status in it, for any tie to a particular person gives him further ties with all its other members. The tie may be of different categories and of varying degrees of kinship. Within the complex of village kinship ties and the circuit of daily contacts all relationships are given equal weight, for what is significant is less the category or degree of kinship than the fact of living together in a small and highly corporate community.

It will be noted that a considerable proportion of the owners of byres in the villages are living there because of affinal relationships,

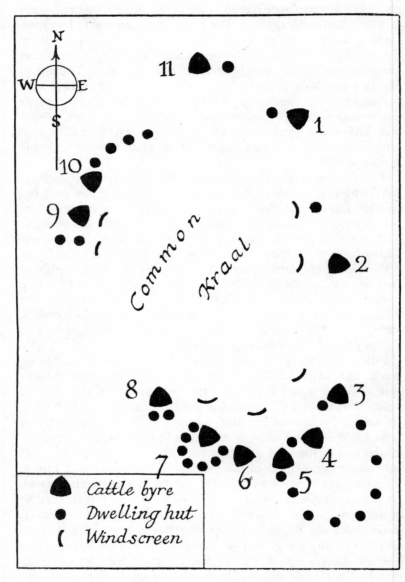

Sketch-map of Konye Village

(10)

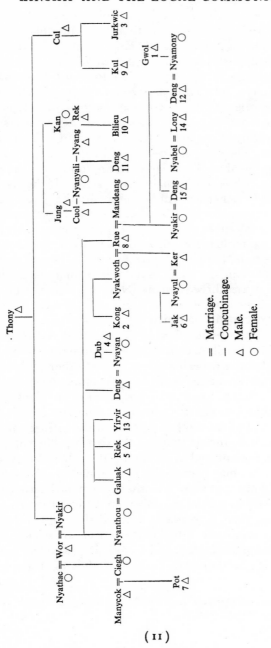

= Marriage.
− Concubinage.
△ Male.
○ Female.

KONYE VILLAGE

(11)

and I must here say again that although *mar* is properly kinship traced through father or mother, long-standing affinal relationships count in Nuer eyes as being equal to kinship, being a kind of kinship through the children of marriage unions, especially when the affinal relatives live together, as so many of them do at Konye. As a Nuer at another village, Kurmayom on the Sobat river, put it: 'Well, you have seen my home and the people who live here; are they not the husbands of my sisters? Well, all our cattle are exhausted from giving them to our brothers-in-law. They are our people and form part of our community (*cieng*) Nyabor. Their children are known by the names of their mothers while they remain in our village. If they go to the homes of their fathers they will be known by the names of their fathers'. Affines may therefore be regarded in a general social sense as *mar* and we may speak of Konye community as a cluster of kin.

My second example is the village of Nyueny in the Leek tribal territory of western Nuerland. I spent five weeks there in 1936. The village is spread along the arc of a sandy ridge for about a mile and a half. It comprises three hamlets, Nyueny, Dakyil, and Kamthiang, and about a mile to the north of it lies the hamlet of Dhorpan, the occupants of which used to form part of the main village. In 1936 the population of Nyueny was reckoned to be about 130 souls, distributed in twenty-six homesteads. As I had already recorded the genealogical pattern of other Nuer villages and camps I did not aim at drawing up a complete genealogy for Nyueny, but rather at a survey of domestic unions. Consequently the kinship links between the owners of four homesteads (numbers 1, 5, 22, and 26) and other persons in the village cannot be stated. This merely means that the relationship did not emerge from an inquiry conducted to other ends than their discovery, for links of some kind may confidently be assumed to exist. It should also be pointed out that there are other connexions between some of the persons whose names are shown on the chart which are not indicated there, though they are recorded elsewhere,* and there may be others unknown to me. Only persons significant for the present discussion are tabled, and I have simplified the presentation by treating ghost-marriages as though they were simple legal marriages.

* 'Some Aspects of Marriage and the Family among the Nuer', *Rhodes–Livingstone Paper* No. 11, 1945, pp. 29 ff.

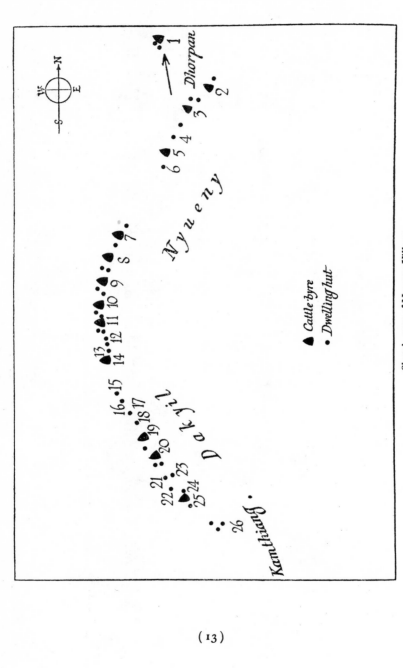

Sketch-map of Nyueny Village

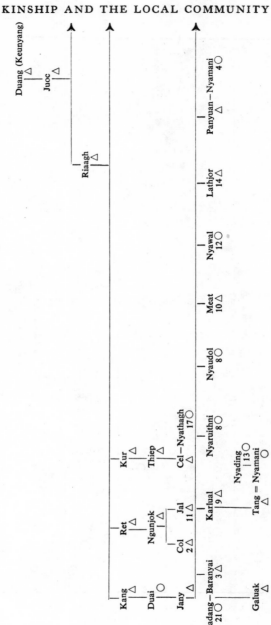

NYUENY VILLAGE

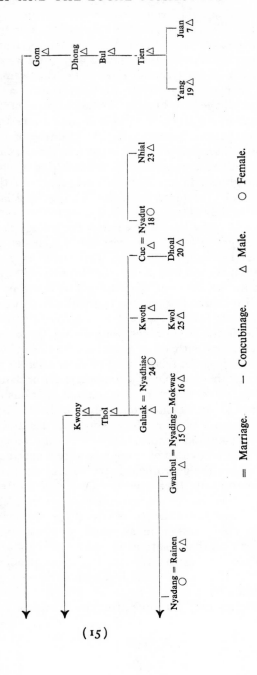

= Marriage.　　— Concubinage.　　△ Male.　　○ Female.

(15)

The village site belongs to the Riaagh lineage of the Keunyang maximal lineage of the Gaatbol clan, the dominant clan in Leek tribal area of which Karlual area, where Nyueny is situated, is a section. Members of that lineage with their wives and concubines and their affines account for ten out of the twenty-six homesteads. The people of Nyueny hamlet, the central and northern parts of the village, are known as 'the children of Jany', and Jany's descendants with their wives and concubines and affines account for another ten homesteads. 'The children of Jany', whose *tut* is Karlual (homestead 9), count collectively as *gaatwac*, children of the paternal aunt, or, as Nuer often put it, *gaatnyiet*, children of daughters, to the Riaagh lineage, whom they call *gaatnar*, children of the maternal uncle. The senior Riaagh men are the 'bulls' of the village in the tribal sense of the word *tut*.

It will again be observed that the village is not an exclusive lineage group (with its wives) but is a cluster of kin (including affines). In this case, however, there is a lineage core to the village community, and this core is that branch of the dominant clan of the tribe which owns the village site. Some members of its collateral minimal lineage, the Gom, also live in the village. I draw attention to further typical features. We saw that at Konye many of the heads of families were living there because of affinal relationships with other members of the village. The counterpart to this is the relationship of sister's son to mother's brother, for when the children of a resident sister or daughter grow up in a village those who stand in an affinal relationship to their father stand in an avuncular relationship to them. This is a very significant feature of Nuer local communities and from it follows another common feature: in course of time a maternal link of this kind may be treated as though it were a paternal link and therefore within the genealogical structure of the principal lineage of the community. Jany's mother Duai is so treated. Nuer say of a woman who has this structural position that 'she has become a man'. Cognation becomes regarded for ordinary social purposes within community life as equal to agnation. A sister's son—mother's brother relationship may come about in a village not by a man going to live with his wife's people but by widows bringing their children to live with their own people after their husbands have died, a mode of residence which in certain circumstances may continue after the deaths of the mothers. This is illustrated at Nyueny by the daughters of Jany. The widows may take lovers in the village, or they may take them from a different village and their lovers come to live with them. This custom is another feature of interest, for some ties between members of a village may be through widow-concubines, or even through unmarried concubines. Any such ties are *mar*, kinship.

Allowing for the fact I have mentioned, that when people live together as members of the same small local community female links are often given equivalence to male links in a genealogy, a cluster of kin such as that of Nyueny can be presented as descended from a common ancestor. It might be described as a cognatic lineage, but in speaking of the Nuer I think it wise to restrict the term 'lineage' to a group of agnates within a system of such groups and to speak of a cluster like that of Nyueny as being a lineage to which are attached, on account of common residence, other lines of kin through females. For if an attached family or extended family of this kind were to leave the common residence the link which binds them to the lineage would cease to be significant for them and would lose its importance in favour of some new link more appropriate to their new attachment, whatever that might be, in their new village. Within a cluster of this kind relations between persons are regulated by the values of the kinship system. Seen as a unit from the outside, and in its corporate relations with other village communities, lineage values are dominant.

I now examine the kinship texture of a cattle camp at which I resided for close on three months in 1931. Yakwac is a small mound on the left bank of the Sobat. Like Nyueny, it is on the periphery of Nuerland where the Lou tribe faces the small Balak Dinka people who at one time occupied both banks of the river. I should explain that it was necessity rather than choice which led me to spend a large part of my time among the Lou Nuer at peripheral points. As I had no land transport and the Lou could not be induced to act as porters I had to rely on transport by canoe, and the larger rivers are in many places the tribal frontiers.

Yakwac village consists—I speak of 1931—of only three byres and a few attached huts. The chief man of the village is Cam-Carau, who owns one of the byres, the other two being owned by Bithou, his brother, and Kirkir, a kinsman of his mother. The real 'bull' of the village is, however, Cam's mother, Nyagen, and the village is often spoken of as *cieng* Nyagen. She has what amounts to the honorary status of a man, not only on account of her age and kinship status, but also, and principally, because she is a Lou aristocrat and it is through her that Cam and his family link themselves on to the dominant lineage of the area in which they live, for Cam is a Jikany tribesman and, although an aristocrat in his own tribal territory, a stranger in the Lou country. He married his first wife to the name of his maternal uncle, Dar, with Dar's

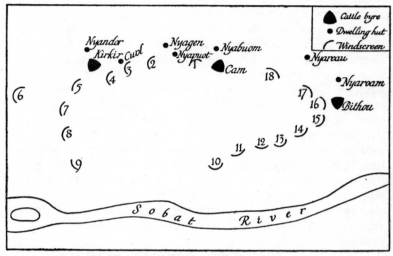

Sketch-map of Yakwac Cattle Camp

cattle, so that his eldest son and the other children born of this wife count as Dar's children and not as his own; and as Dar and Cam are of different clans and tribes, the distinction between pater and genitor is emphasized. His eldest son, Wia, belongs to the dominant clan of the Lou territory and he does not.

In many years Cam's maternal kinsmen, the minor lineage known as *cieng* Pual, the community (of the descendants) of Puol, come during the dry season to water and pasture their cattle and to fish and bathe at Yakwac from their inland village of Majok in the Nyerol district. This minor lineage has four branches—the minimal lineages of Diel, Malual, Kwoth, and Mar—members of all of which figure in the genealogy of the camp.

The entire population of Majok was not at Yakwac in 1931, for many of its members, including most of the womenfolk, had remained inland and some families spent the dry season at other camps on the Sobat. The women who came to Yakwac slept in the huts of the village, so no grass beehive huts were erected. The population of the camp was about eighty souls. I have again simplified the genealogy by showing ghost-marriages as simple legal marriages, but I have indicated, as I have not done in the other genealogies presented in this chapter, those members of the camp who are known to be Dinka or of Dinka descent. Those among them who are shown as members of the Pual lineage have been adopted into one of its branches. The names of only a few women and none of small children are given in the genealogical table, which is intended to demonstrate the kinship ties between the occupants of the windscreens, all of whom, with the exception of the mother of Cam, are males.

A study of the genealogy of Yakwac cattle camp reveals the features we have already noted as being significant in the genealogy of Nyueny. It is a lineage structure—the lineage being a branch of the dominant clan in the tribal area and that branch which is dominant in the district in which the camp was formed—to which are attached other lines through females, thus giving the genealogy a cognatic form, and affines. In order to graft themselves on to the tree of this dominant clan the linked families trace their descent through females at the points of graft as though these women had been men. It was a long time before I discovered, for example, that Kirkir's paternal grandfather was Buom and not Kol. A rather unusual example in which this process is strikingly illustrated is the line of ascent of Deng-Nyajal through females in three generations to the point of graft, Gai. Nyanhial and her daughter Nyajal were captured by the Anuak on a raid into Lou country and for many years lived in Anuakland, where Deng was begotten by an Anuak father. In the camp Deng was always referred to as Deng-Nyajal after his mother and not as Deng-Cul after his father, because Nyajal, and not Cul, is genealogically significant in Deng's social milieu. In the same way we referred always to Cuol as Cuol-Mer and not as Cuol-Rwac. In this cluster of kin at Yakwac camp the importance of affinal and maternal ties is evident.

I have indicated Dinka origins, where I have satisfactory evidence for them, partly to show the very considerable absorption of Dinka which has taken place, by adoption into Nuer lineages and through marriage, in a typical Nuer community, and partly to account for some marriages which might otherwise appear to be breaches of the Nuer rules of exogamy. These Dinka are of varied tribal origin. Among those whose names appear in the genealogy I have recorded Bor, Fadang, Luac, Thoc, and Dunjol origins. The absorption of so many Dinka has affected, through the practice of adoption, the rules regulating marriage, and it has also affected modes of residence, since a Dinka who has not been adopted into a Nuer lineage readily attaches himself to his wife's people or to the people who have married his sister or daughter, as do also his children to their maternal uncle's kin. The absorption of Dinka has led to a further complication in the already very complicated patterns of Nuer genealogies, for it sometimes happens that captured Dinka brothers or other kin are adopted into different lineages or even into different clans.

I would also draw attention to the different tribal origins of those Nuer in the genealogy who are not members of the dominant lineage, because they illustrate the movement of individuals and families which is so characteristic a feature of Nuer society: Yit was a Bul tribesman, he and Pinien being children of sisters or, as the Nuer say, a man and his *gatmanlende*, his mother's sister's son; Carau and Wan-Wang were Jikany tribesmen, Carau being an aristocrat of the Lony section of the Jikany, though begotten by an Anuak; Nhial-Deng is of Thiang tribal origin; Kurcam was a man of the Jimem clan, a clan which is found throughout Nuerland and without a tribal territory of its own; and so forth. Indeed, it is necessary to point out that not all outsiders attached to a lineage core remain attached to it. Nuer move about their country freely, and reside for some years with one lot of kin and then for some years with another.

The genealogy of Yakwac camp gives us a typical cross-section of a Nuer tribal society. We see how the local community is built up around a lineage through attachment to it of extra-lineage persons by the stressing of one or other category of kinship, and we thus see further the relation of the lineage structure to the kinship system within the framework of the tribal society. The collateral, and in a structural sense, opposed lineage to the Pual is the Dumien, who live near Pul Thul and Pul Nyerol in the same Nyerol district in which the Pual have their wet-season home and who, like them, often camp on the Sobat river in the drought. A genealogical analysis of the Dumien community would disclose the same kind of cluster as has been disclosed for the Pual community—a *thok dwiel*, lineage, to which are linked in many different ways through kinship values *rul*, strangers, and *jang*, Dinka, the whole forming a *cieng*, a local community who are kin. Pual and Dumien together form a single major lineage called Leng, the collateral to which is the Nyarkwac lineage whose home is adjacent to the home of the Leng. The Nyarkwac lineage in its community form consists of similar clusters composed of its branches and their accretions. Leng and Nyarkwac lineages form the Gaatbal maximal lineage, occupying the northern part of the Lou tribal territory and one of the three maximal lineages of the Jinaca clan, which is the dominant clan of the Lou tribe.

My final illustration is included to draw special attention to natural, as contrasted with what we may call legal, ties of kinship in Nuer society. These are brought about by unions other than the union of simple legal marriage and are very numerous in Nuerland. I explain their nature in Chapter III. The recognition of natural ties in the Nuer system of kinship values as social ties, and not merely as natural relationships, further enhances the significance of women as persons through whom descent is traced for the purpose of establishing kinship with those with whom Nuer have relations in their community life.

I quoted earlier in this chapter a remark made to me by a Nuer of Kurmayom, where I spent about three weeks in 1931. Kurmayom is a village of the Lou tribe to the west of Yakwac and, like it, on the Sobat river. It is near the border between the Lou tribe and the Ngok Dinka. The most prominent person in the village is a noted magician called Bul-Kan, and it is his family that I shall now briefly examine. He and the cluster of kin around him occupy eleven byres in the chief hamlet of the village. He is a member of a minimal lineage called (*cieng*) Nyabor after the name of his mother's mother. She was a woman of the Nyarkwac major lineage of the Jinaca clan who bore her children in unmarried concubinage to two men. The fathers legitimatized their children by payment of cattle. Lim, Nyawin, and Tonydeang thus became members of the Jidiet clan since their pater, called Kwaclath, was a man of this clan, and Gir, Thakjaak, and Nyanhial became members of the Jimem clan, their pater Bilieu being a man of this clan. One of these children, the girl Nyawin, married Kan-Kwoth of the Kiek clan, to whom she bore Yuth, Nyakong, and Nyatony before he died. She continued to live in his home after his death and there took a lover, a man of the Ngok Dinka called Cie, to whom she bore Bul, Nyang, and Mun. These three sons count, of course, as children of Kan-Kwoth. The Dinka Cie then, at the behest of Nyawin and her sons, took a wife to himself with cattle of the herd of Kan-Kwoth and by her begat Yual. Yual was therefore not only a natural paternal half-brother of Bul, Nyang, and Mun but also their brother in a further sense, for he was *gat ghokien*, the child of their cattle. I was told that he had also been formally adopted by Bul into his lineage. Mun had died before 1931, and Bul and Nyang were already elderly men whose sons and daughters had homes and herds and children of their own.

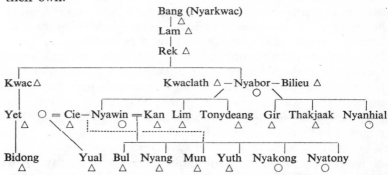

It will be noted that, although Bul is called after his father Kan and is a member of the Kiek clan and his mother was a woman of the Jidiet clan, the lineage now call themselves *cieng* Nyabor and trace their ascent through Nyabor into the stem of the Nyarkwac branch of the dominant Jinaca clan, neglecting for ordinary social purposes the lines of descent of both Kan and Kwaclath. They attach themselves in this way to the lineage which owns the village site and with whom the tribal section in which it is situated is identified, its chief 'bull' in the village being Bidong-Yet, whose name I have therefore inserted in the table.

IV

The kinship relations of persons to one another in a Nuer community are, I think it will be agreed, very complex. Indeed they are more complex than I have shown them to be so far, as will appear when the forms of domestic union obtaining among the Nuer are described. The complexity is partly due to these diverse forms of marriage, and also to the python-like assimilation by the Nuer of vast numbers of Dinka through adoption or inter-marriage.

However, certain preliminary conclusions of a general kind can be drawn from the few genealogies—only a fraction of those col-lected—I have cited as examples. A Nuer community, whether small or big, is not composed exclusively of members of a single lineage and their wives or, correspondingly, not all members of a lineage live in the same community. On the other hand, in any large village or camp there is represented an agnatic lineage of one or other order and into the growth of this lineage are grafted, through the tracing of descent through females, branches which are regarded in certain situations and in a certain sense as part of it and in other situations and in a different sense as not part of it. Other lines and persons are grafted into the lineage by adoption, but this can only happen to Dinka and other foreigners, not to men of true Nuer origin. Attached to the lineage, directly or indirectly, are also a considerable number of affines of diverse kinds.

In their collective relations with other communities, and as seen collectively by the members of these communities, there is a fusion of the attached elements with the lineage. They are incor-porated in it, and the resultant whole is spoken of as the *cieng* or *wec*, community, of the lineage, which is both its core and the symbol of its social identity as a unit in the tribal system. But within the community itself there are occasions when a formal distinction between the lineage and its incorporated elements has to be made and the status of its members has to be defined to the exclusion of the *rul*, strangers: the *gaatnyiet*, the children of daughters (of the lineage), and the affines.

In daily contacts between persons within the community their relations are expressed not in the language of lineage structure but in the language of the kinship system by reference to categories of kinship within that system. Thus men of the same minimal lineage have only an undifferentiated lineage relationship on such occasions as the lineage acts or is thought of as a group. Otherwise, and as persons, their relationship to one another is one of *gwanlen*, father's brother, *gatgwanlen*, father's brother's son, *wac*, father's sister, and so on.

Lineages are articulated as groups of agnatic kin at a different, usually ritual, level of the social life, and they are articulated as conglomerates, fused with other elements, at the political level. Kinship ties belong to another order of social relations, relations between persons and not between groups. The members of a lineage group are socially undifferentiated as such in the inter-lineage structure because it is a structural relationship between groups. In the kinship system they are socially differentiated by category and degree of relationship—this being an essential characteristic of the system—because the kinship system is a system of relationships between persons.

As we have seen, members of a Nuer community are all *mar*, kin (including affines in this term), to one another. Whoever is kith must also be kin. Common membership of a village or camp does not in itself provide a man with a secure basis for his personal relations with its other members. That is provided chiefly by the kinship system by which a kinship tie established with any person in the village or camp gives a man a kinship status of some kind with every other person in the village or camp—with all his neigh-bours. Consequently a local community consists of a great number of cross-strands which compose an intricate network of kinship ties.

The relationships which enter into any particular composition are not the same as those of another, and they change from year to year and from season to season inasmuch as Nuer frequently change their place of residence. Therefore a cluster of kin of this kind does not constitute a specific kinship group. When it is thought of by Nuer as a unit it is not as a kinship group but as a residential group by association with a lineage or site. Its mem-bers are *jicieng* so-and-so, the people of a community of a certain lineage, or *ji* such-and-such, the people of a certain place. To any member of the community the rest are '*jiciengda*', 'the people of my home'. '*Jimarida*', 'my kin', has quite a different connotation: it is a set of personal relationships to him and includes men and women who do not belong to the cluster at all.

The absorption of Dinka into these communities of kin on so considerable a scale has been significant. As I have pointed out in *The Nuer*, assimilation of conquered Dinka tribes and tribal sec-tions has not, for various reasons, resulted in a class or caste, or in

(24)

1. A boy, clothed in ashes

any other rigid hierarchical structure. It has been brought about by their incorporation into Nuer lineages by adoption and by their assimilation to them through intermarriage. When Dinka are adopted into a lineage, absorption into Nuer society presents no great difficulty. Their Dinka origin is remembered by members of the lineage of their adoption, at any rate for some generations, but after one or two generations it may not be known to outsiders; and I suppose that in course of time it may be forgotten within the lineage itself. They are part of the lineage, have the same status as its other members, and are points of growth in the branch equal to men born into it. But when Dinka are not adopted into a Nuer lineage absorption is achieved with greater difficulty and by circuitous means. If we examine closely the history of those persons in the genealogies I have recorded who have attached themselves permanently to an affinal or maternal family and through it to a minimal lineage, and if we trace also the histories of those persons who through such an attachment in the past now trace their descent from the lineage through a female, we shall find that in a very great number, I venture to say in the vast majority, of cases they are Dinka. This is a development which it is easy to understand because captured Dinka or Dinka immigrants into Nuerland have lost their status in their own kinship and lineage systems, and if they are not adopted into Nuer lineages they can only acquire status in Nuer society through affinal relationships; and their children, having no kin on the father's side, identify themselves with the mother's kin and, having no lineage on the father's side, seek affiliation to the mother's lineage. It is true that we find strangers of Nuer clans as members of clusters of kin around a lineage core of the dominant clan of the tribe, but where the attachment is permanent these strangers are, in my experience, generally persons of those Nuer clans which have no tribal territory of their own—no *wec*, local community, as Nuer say— like the Jimem, Jikul, and Kiek clans. These clans have, moreover, in some cases mythological beginnings placing them outside the main family of Nuer clans and suggesting foreign origin. Assimilation in such cases can never be so complete as in the case of Dinka, because members of Nuer clans have their own clan symbols and their own *buth* relationships which attach them to the lineages of their birth.

Another factor which has certainly had some influence in

bringing about attachments of outsiders to groups of agnatic kin other than their own is the custom of concubinage, the different forms of which I describe in detail later. It is a very common practice for widows to leave their dead husbands' homes and to take lovers in the villages of their parents, or to go to reside in the villages of their lovers. When they do so they take their young children with them, and though the sons almost invariably return to their paternal homes before initiation, they have grown up in the homes of their maternal kinsmen, or of their foster fathers' kin, and may have so strong an affection for them that they later return to reside with them, at any rate for a time, when they are married men and their own masters.

Widows, whether living in their maternal villages or in their dead husbands' villages, attract lovers, sometimes from the village, sometimes from a neighbouring village. In either case a new social tie is established, and the lovers may continue to cohabit with the widows as members of their communities for long periods and nurture the children they beget by them. A poor man is only too glad to obtain a housekeeper and mate without expense by means of either widow-concubinage or unmarried concubinage, and if he is an unadopted Dinka he may remain with the concubine and his children by her.

There are in Nuerland a considerable number of unmarried concubines. The sons they bear to lovers become the legal children of these lovers by payment of cattle, but they do not feel so securely attached to the homes of their fathers as do children born of the union of marriage, and there is a tendency for sons of the same woman by different fathers to stick together, usually wherever their mother may be, especially if the fathers are dead or if they do not possess large herds.

There are two other facts to be taken into consideration. Among Nuer it is not uncommon for a man to make his home among his wife's people, though in my experience a true Nuer usually returns to his own people eventually. As I have explained, sons-in-law who live with their wives' people are often Dinka, and Dinka are likely to remain with their affines, as they may have no kin of their own to return to; but one also finds Nuer in the same position. These may be persons who for one reason or another prefer to live apart from their paternal kin, or they may be poor men who cannot afford to pay the full bridewealth, part of which is forgone by the wife's family in view of the fact that the man who has married their daughter has joined their community and is bringing up his children as members of it. They may even give him some of their own cattle to help him build up a herd. The second fact to be taken into consideration is the Nuer custom, for various reasons not always observed, by which the eldest child of a marriage is brought up by his, or her, maternal grandparents. A child brought up in his maternal kinsmen's village naturally feels that in some respects it, and not his paternal kinsmen's village, is his home.

Cattle are a powerful element, often the deciding consideration, especially in the minds of unadopted Dinka captives or immigrants, in a man's choice of residence. A Nuer cannot live for long without cattle, and he who possesses none must attach himself to the byre and herd of some kinsman. Men with only a few beasts also sometimes find it a convenience to tether them in the byre of a kinsman rather than build a byre of their own. One often finds that the reason a man decides to live with one of his maternal kin, with a paternal aunt, with one of his affinal kin, or with the family of a widow-concubine, is that he knows that the person he intends to reside with will allow him to be a member of the household, will give shelter to his animals if he has any, and will help him to start a herd if he lacks cattle entirely; whereas his paternal kinsmen are unable or unwilling to do so, or, in the case of many Dinka, are altogether absent.

As a further conclusion, I remark again that the drawing together by, and into, the lineage system of the many different strands of kinship (and affinity) which compose the network of social ties in each local community gives the community its unitary character and fixes its position in tribal structure. The points at which they are drawn together are the 'bulls' of the kinship clusters, and especially the tribal 'bulls', those men who are persons not only of age, wealth, and character, but also members of the dominant clan of the tribe—tribal aristocrats. These tribal 'bulls' are the centres of clusters of kin, but they are also agnates, and each has in relation to the others a structural position in the lineage system of the dominant clan. Through them, therefore, all the tribesmen are attached to the dominant clan of the tribe and all the local communities are assimilated to the highly consistent structure of its segments, in which they are conceptualized. It is the ambition of every man, of the dominant clan especially, to become a 'bull' and the centre of a cluster of kin, and Nuer say that it is for this reason among others that families often break up and cousins and brothers part, each to seek to gather his own community around him.

I suggest that it is the clear, consistent, and deeply rooted lineage structure of the Nuer which permits persons and families to move about and attach themselves so freely, for shorter or longer periods, to whatever community they choose by whatever cognatic or affinal tie they find it convenient to emphasize; and that it is on account of the firm values of the structure that this flux does not cause confusion or bring about social disintegration. It would seem it may be partly just because the agnatic principle is unchallenged in Nuer society that the tracing of descent through women is so prominent and matrilocality so prevalent. However much the actual configurations of kinship clusters may vary and change, the lineage structure is invariable and stable.

CHAPTER II

MARRIAGE PROHIBITIONS AND INCEST

I

WE noticed in the last chapter that local clusters of kin comprise persons of different clans and of different tribal origins and that, moreover, they are not fixed compositions. Their members, individuals and families, move often and freely, going to stay, seasonally or for many years, with different kinsmen in other villages and camps, generally, though not always, in the same tribal area. Wherever they go they are easily incorporated into the new community through one or more kinship links. Apart from such moves, Nuer frequently visit all the villages in their neighbourhood, and in all of them they have kinsfolk. I have demonstrated the network of kinship ties in selected local communities, but we have to think of all the different strands of relationship in each community passing outside it and across the bush to link its members to those of other communities. I am not speaking here of lineage ties, but of ties of kinship or personal relationship. Consequently the different local communities of a whole tribe could be presented on a single genealogical chart. Given unlimited time and patience, the entire population of Nuerland could be so presented. There are no closed communities. Villages and camps are spatially separated, but they merge into one another socially through a multitude of cross-strands of kinship between persons as well as forming parts of a single political structure.

This wide acknowledgement of kinship might be expected to be found together, as it is, with a wide range of marriage prohibitions, which have the effect of spreading the marriages of members of any local group and creating innumerable links through women between persons in many different communities. In view of what we have already learnt about the place of maternal and affinal ties in kinship configurations, we shall also not be surprised to discover that relationships of both kinds are covered by marriage prohibitions outside the rules of clan exogamy.

It is these marriage prohibitions I now propose to examine. I discuss the subject of incest at the same time because, although the rules forbidding marriage within certain groups and between certain categories of persons are not coterminous with those forbidding sexual congress, the two cannot be divorced. The reason given by Nuer for their marriage prohibitions is that were marriage to take place within certain degrees of relationship it would be *rual*, incest.

The word *rual* means both incest and the misfortune which it causes. Syphilis and certain forms of yaws are believed to be especially a consequence of incest, though retribution may come in any form, from wild beasts, a spear, drowning, sickness, &c. These misfortunes can sometimes be avoided by sacrifice. On the other hand, they may fall not only on the partners to the sin but also on their closest relatives, so that a man who commits incest may render himself responsible for homicide as well.

When it is forbidden for a man to have relations with a woman he may not, of course, marry her, and it will be simpler to begin this account by stating the Nuer table of marriage prohibitions. Marriage is not permitted between clansfolk, close cognates, close natural kinsfolk, close kinsfolk by adoption, close affines, and persons who stand to one another as fathers and daughters in the age-set system.

A man may not marry a clanswoman and *a fortiori* a woman of his lineage. Agnatic kinship is recognized between some clans, but it does not constitute a bar to intermarriage. The relationship is considered to be very distant and, in any case, the ancestor of the fraternal clans is believed to have cut an ox in twain to permit intermarriage between the descendants of his sons. Nuer accept the hypothesis that maximal lineages of the larger clans might one day split apart and marriage be allowed between them, but 'at present they are too close'. They say '*cike diel*', 'they have not yet reached ten generations (from their founder)'. They perceive that the limits of clan exogamy have been fixed arbitrarily and are not unalterable.

Clan exogamy is stated by Nuer in terms of clan symbols. Each clan has one or more spear-names, with which go certain honorific titles, and the spear-names of the bride's clan and the bridegroom's clan are formally shouted out at weddings. They must not be exactly the same, for this would mean that the marriage was a breach of the rule of clan exogamy. When a marriage is proposed between a youth and maid whose families are strangers the first inquiry made is into the spear-names of their clans. It sometimes happens that two unrelated clans have the same primary spear-names but have different secondary spear-names which serve to distinguish them ritually. It also sometimes happens that two maximal lineages of the same clan have different secondary spear-names, but in this case the secondary differentiation would not permit intermarriage. Nuer go into this matter very carefully if there is any doubt about clan relationship, as in certain circumstances there might be.

A man may not marry any close cognate. Nuer consider that if relationship can be traced between a man and a woman through either father or mother, however many female links there may be, up to six generations, though the number of generations is not absolutely fixed, marriage should not take place between them. An ox is believed to have been cut in two in ancient days to permit intermarriage between persons who are descended from a common ancestor beyond that point, so long as they are not agnates. Nuer explain that a man who is related to a woman as far back as six generations might still claim a small gift at her marriage, a clear indication that they cannot marry. If a proposed union is a borderline case a gourd may be ritually broken in half to end kinship. They then say 'bakena mar', 'we split kinship', and 'ba bak ne kir', 'it (kinship) is split with a gourd'. It should be noted, however, that a man cannot marry the daughter of a woman of his own maximal lineage even though the lines of himself and the mother converge at a point more than six generations back. Some clans permit marriage to the daughter of a woman of a collateral maximal lineage of the clan. Stated in a slightly different way, a man or woman may marry into his, or her, mother's clan but not into her maximal lineage. Other clans do not allow a man to marry into his mother's clan in any circumstances.

When, as often happens among the Nuer, the physiological father, the genitor, is a different man from the legal father, the pater, his sons will not marry into his minimal lineage because the physiological connexion is socially recognized by the payment to the natural father of a cow of the bridewealth of his natural daughters. They may, however, marry women of a collateral lineage. Close natural cognation of any kind is a bar to marriage. Thus I was told that a man would not marry the daughter of his *nar laka*, the natural son of his maternal grandfather.

The adoption of a Dinka boy into a Nuer minimal lineage prevents him from marrying into that lineage and he would normally not be allowed to marry into a collateral minimal lineage of the same minor lineage, though such marriages sometimes take place, as is evident in the genealogy of Yakwac cattle camp opposite page 19. Some of my informants were of the opinion that he ought not to marry into the clan at all. If he is permitted to do so, to avoid the appearance of a breach of exogamy, the spear-name *mut jangemo*, spear of this Dinka, is called out in the invocation of the ghosts on the day of his wedding in addition to the clan spear-name which became his by adoption. By this means the spear-names of the bride and bridegroom, which are the same, are distinguished. Also when, as it sometimes happens, a captured Dinka boy is not adopted into his captor's lineage, men of this lineage cannot marry his daughter because some of the cattle of her bridewealth are due to them, since the Dinka will have married with their cattle. The sons of the captor count as paternal uncles in the distribution of her bridewealth, and other members of the lineage may demand gifts from the bridegroom's people.

Captured Dinka girls are not adopted into Nuer lineages and their captors can marry them, though they rarely do so. If the captor of a girl intends to marry her or to let one of his sons marry her he passes a spear-shaft between her legs, and then hands her over to another man to bring up outside his village, 'because if she were to remain in his homestead she would become his daughter'. Generally a captured girl is brought up a member of her captor's household and is regarded as his daughter. He rubs ashes on the back of a sheep and tells his ancestral ghosts that the girl is 'our daughter and our sister'. Nuer say: 'Thus she is taken into the family (*gol*) and becomes a member of the family.' They also say: 'She will become our daughter and we will receive her bridewealth-cattle.' The cattle of her bridewealth give her kinship with the persons among whom it is distributed, as does also her right to receive in return the cows of the paternal aunt on the marriage of the daughters of the sons of her captor and foster-father. Marriage is therefore forbidden between her descendants and the descendants of these kinsmen in virtue of bridewealth for several generations. She herself can be married to a clansman of her foster-father so long as her husband does not belong to his minimal lineage, which is to say so long as those who pay her bridewealth cannot also claim part of it, for those who can claim part of a girl's bride-wealth are kin to her. Nuer state these rules in terms of cattle.

A man may not take his wife's sister or any near kinswoman of his wife as a second wife. A man may be on familiar terms with his wife's sister, but sexual relations with her are incestuous and it is only permissible for him to marry her if his wife has died without having borne children. When I argued that there was no kinship between a man and his wife's sister, Nuer said that this was not true. 'What about the child?' they asked. They regard a man and his wife's sister as related through the child of the wife—for a woman is only fully married when she has a child and comes to live with her husband's people as their 'kinswoman', as they say, since her child is their child. Her sister is therefore also a kind of kinswoman, seeing that she is also the mother of their child. Your wife's sister being your child's maternal aunt is your sister (as we say, sister-in-law). Nuer also define this relationship in terms of cattle. When your daughter is married her mother's sister receives a cow of her bridewealth, and Nuer hold that she cannot both receive this cow and be your wife at the same time, especially as the cow is in some degree regarded as part of the bridewealth still owing from your marriage to your wife. Also, when your wife's sister's daughter marries, your wife will receive a cow and Nuer feel that there is something wrong about this cow coming to her if her sister is also her co-wife. In certain circumstances a woman may claim cattle on her sister's marriage, and in this case the man who pays the cattle would also be the receiver of them were a man to marry his wife's sister—a situation the Nuer regard as impossible. Hence Nuer say that a man may not marry his wife's sister either 'on account of her (the wife's) children' or 'on account of the cattle', which are different ways of saying that he cannot marry his child's maternal aunt. There is a further reason which would prevent a man from marrying his wife's sister while his wife is living, for, as will be explained later, a man may not have sexual relations with two closely related women at the same time. It follows that two brothers ought not to marry sisters or close cousins: 'That would be bad because if your brother died you could not take his wife.'

A man may not marry the daughter of an age-mate, a member of his age-set, 'because she is his daughter'. The blood age-mates have shed together into the ground at their initiation gives them a kind of kinship. In certain circumstances an age-mate may claim a cow, the *yang rica*, of the bridewealth of the daughter of one of his mates and a man may not be in the position of paying bridewealth and being able to claim it. Nuer point out also that were a man to marry the daughter of an age-mate her parents would become his parents-in-law, and the respect he would have to show them would be incompatible with the familiarity with which he should treat age-mates and their wives and the liberties he may take with them. He could not, for instance, eat and drink in their home, an abstention in glaring contradiction to the behaviour expected of age-mates. The prohibition on marriage with the daughter of an age-mate imposes no inconvenience on Nuer, for there would always be a great difference in age between the man and woman, and this is, in any case, an obstacle to marriage seldom surmounted in Nuerland. Strictly speaking, a breach of this prohibition is not *rual* but Nuer say that it is 'like *rual*'. The prohibition is said to have been ordained by God, and it is believed that the guardian spirit of the age-set will avenge a breach of it.

It is said that in the past a man would not have been allowed to marry the daughters of his father's age-mates, for they are in a sense his sisters. It is still not permissible for such a marriage to take place if both the fathers are alive, since this would mean that the two age-mates would enter into a relationship characterized by mutual reserve and in conflict with the egalitarian status of age-mates towards one another. When one of the fathers is dead marriage can take place, but in this case a cow, or more likely a sheep or goat, must be given by each family to the other. This exchange is in payment to the *ric*, the age-set, of the fathers to avoid evil consequences, the animal being called 'the cow of compensation (or atonement) of the age-set'. There is no clash between patterns of behaviour when one of the fathers is dead because the attitudes towards a member of a father's age-set and towards a father-in-law are both of respect.

The rules I have recorded above can be generalized by saying, as Nuer do, that a man may not marry a woman who is *mar*, kin, to him. In the rules prohibiting marriage, kinship is traced farther in some directions than in others and is of different kinds: the clan kinship of the common spear; the *buth* kinship of collateral lineage and of adoption; uterine kinship; kinship through the genitor; the kinship of cognation; kinship which the birth of a child creates between affines; the kinship acknowledged by acceptance of bridewealth; and the kinship by analogy of the age-set.

It will be noted that the wide range of Nuer marriage prohibitions has a certain correspondence with the kinship configuration of their local communities described in the last chapter. The balance there observed between the paternal side and the maternal side in the notion of *mar*, kinship, and its reflection in residential attachments is seen again in the conventions governing marriage. The assimilation of affinal to kinship ties, noted as significant in the local network of relationships, is also a significant feature of these conventions. The rules taken as a whole amount to this: a man must not marry kin (including affines), and as he is born and brought up in a circle of kin which normally embraces the people of his immediate neighbourhood, he is generally compelled to marry outside it. He is also compelled to look for sweethearts outside it; and I think that this is one reason why Nuer youths like to stay in the villages and camps of maternal and affinal relatives where they have greater freedom in sexual matters.

Nevertheless, however extensive the prohibitions may be, there must always be a point in each category of them at which a marriage can just be allowed or is just disallowed. In these borderline cases there is some latitude in interpretation of the prohibitions. Cases arise in which there is disagreement whether the genealogical distance between a suitor and the girl whom he wishes to marry is wide enough to permit marriage. It sometimes happens also that a girl's family raise an objection on the score of relationship that they would not have raised had they been better disposed towards the marriage. Indeed, this is a common way of telling a suitor politely that his suit is unwelcome—even when, in fact, there is no relationship which could be seriously urged against the union. It also happens that a distant relationship, which might have been adduced as a bar to marriage, is passed over by a girl's family if they consider the suitor a desirable son-in-law. I have been present at marriage negotiations when a kinsman, who was not satisfied with his share of the bridewealth, raised the objection of kinship, and later, when satisfied, waived it; and at another marriage when one kinsman of the bride urged that the union would be incestuous, while the other kinsmen held that it would not be so. When marriage is permitted in borderline cases of this kind a beast will generally be sacrificed to cut what kinship there may be held still to be between the partners to the union. This is done because it is feared that otherwise the marriage may not be fruitful.

In doubtful cases it may be taken into consideration that some of the links between the pair are those of adoption or of ghost-parentage and not of consanguinity. Also, if there is some doubt about the correctness of a union it is sometimes held to be less questionable if the bride and bridegroom do not belong to the same local community.

Exceptions to the general principles governing marriage prohibitions do not invalidate them, for the rules are acknowledged even in the breach of them. Thus I have known of a peculiar marriage into the clan in which, on the day of the wedding, tribute was paid to the prohibition on intra-clan marriage by omitting the traditional calling out of the spear-names of bride and bridegroom at the invocation of the ghosts.*

The prohibitions of marriage I have related apply also to con-cubinary unions. The *concubinus* and *concubina* ought not to be related in any of the ways I have mentioned, though here there seems to be greater laxity than in matrimonial unions. Concu-binage is entered into on the initiative of the partners to the union and without the public discussion matrimony entails, so that distant, but nevertheless valid, kinship may escape notice. My reason for believing that this is so is that I came across several cases where the death of the children born in concubinage led to a fuller investigation which revealed relationship, of which the partners were ignorant, and consequently to the dissolution of their partnership.

II

It is not incestuous for a man to have relations with daughters of men of his father's age-set and he would not hesitate to make love to them. In all other cases where it is forbidden for a man to marry a woman standing in a certain relationship to him it is also

---

* The husband was the son of a man of the Gaatnaca clan but had been begotten in ghost-marriage by his pater's sister's son, a man of the Gaatgankir clan. The wife's pater was a woman of the Gaatnaca clan (of a different lineage). She had married a wife to raise up children to herself by an unrelated man. The marriage could not have taken place had the wife's pater been a man. As it was, it was subjected to criticism. The reader will understand these peculiar cir-cumstances better after he has read Chapter III.

forbidden to him to be intimate with her, though the prohibition has not always the same force or extension. Before discussing the different degrees of seriousness with which Nuer view breaches of the various rules, I will mention the other relationships which carry the incest taboo besides those, already recorded, which exclude marriage either absolutely or contingently.

Nuer consider it to be *rual* for a man to have relations with wives of any close living kinsmen, except, as is explained later, wives of some paternal kinsmen. The worst incest of this kind is with wives of the father, uterine brother, son, and maternal uncle. It is considered almost as bad as relations with the sister and entails the same consequences. Relations with the mother's co-wife (father's wife) are thought to be shocking because the father has relations with her and afterwards with the mother carrying the son's contact with the co-wife to the mother. It is also *rual* to have relations with wives of the sons of the maternal uncle and of the paternal and maternal aunts. Relations with wives of affines, such as a second wife of the sister's husband, are also regarded as incestuous. It is only congress with wives of the paternal uncles, paternal half-brothers, and paternal cousins which are spoken of without opprobrium. The worst that is said about congress with wives of these kinsmen is that it is a *rual ma tot*, a slight incest, which will not injure the partners to it. It might harm the women's babies, but it is thought that even this penalty can be avoided easily and without expense by cutting in twain, in the place of an animal sacrifice, a *kwol*, a wild yellow tomato-like fruit found in abundance near habitations. It is only if the paternal uncle is the father's uterine brother or if his family form a common household with that of the father that relations with his wife are regarded in a more serious light. They may bring on the offenders serious misfortunes.

The uterine brother is a brother *kwi man*, on the mother's side, and the thought of relations with his wife evokes the disgust Nuer feel at any association of sex with the mother. They regard relations with wives of relatives of the mother's side with distaste 'because of the mother'. The uterine paternal uncle partakes, in a lesser degree, of the same maternal associations because he is a son of the father's mother. But the paternal half-uncles, the paternal half-brothers, and the paternal cousins are 'bulls', and '*Tut thilke rual*', 'There is no incest among bulls'. If they live in different villages from that of the adulterer some compensation in cattle might be exacted, but if they live in the same village it will not be asked for: 'There would be no compensation, for they are of the same community (*cieng*).' Nuer say, however, that adultery with the wife of a paternal half-uncle is wrong 'because of the father', which means because the half-uncle should be treated with the respect due to the father. To have relations with his wife is not incestuous but shows lack of deference. Relations with the wives of paternal half-brothers and paternal cousins are not subject to the same restraint. It is not *rual* to have relations with the wife of an age-mate, but it is regarded as a grave breach of confidence, for a man will trust his wife to the honour of an age-mate, and it is believed that the guardian spirit of the age-set will punish the offender.

It is forbidden on incestuous grounds to have relations with wives of kinsmen, other than those mentioned, only during their lifetime, when they are themselves cohabiting with their wives. It is permissible, indeed to some extent obligatory, to take the places of the husbands in leviratic marriage. It is usual for a widow to cohabit with her dead husband's brother. Rarely a son takes her, and occasionally a sister's son. If a man thus cohabits with his father's, brother's, or maternal uncle's widow he first breaks off the physical relationship between the widow and her late spouse by sacrificing a sheep. Nuer say: 'He divides them with a sheep.' 'The father (or brother, or maternal uncle) is removed', as they say, not so much, if at all, because there would be any danger of *rual*, but in order to be rid of any evil the dead man might have had in his heart towards the man who is taking his wife which might injure her or her children. If a living father or brother gives up a wife to his son or brother, as occasionally happens, a similar sacrifice has to be made, but here the notion of *rual* is more pronounced.

The prohibition on a man having relations with a kinsman's wife is part of a more general regulation which forbids, as *rual*, two close kinsmen to have relations with the same woman, though, here again, 'bulls' do not come, altogether or to some extent, under the ban. Likewise, two closely related women must not have relations with the same man. Nuer youths are careful to inquire of a girl, if they are uncertain of her affairs, whether she has a sweetheart among their close kinsmen. A man may, however, start an affair with a girl as soon as a kinsman has broken off relations with her. This rule, which refers to courtship and sweethearts rather than to casual intercourse, applies to father and son, uterine brothers, and to a lesser degree paternal half-brothers, and also in some degree to cousins, except to paternal parallel cousins, for they are 'bulls' and it does not matter if they share sweethearts. The prohibition is, however, only forcibly enunciated with regard to kinsfolk who are also members of the same village. Hence it is said that it is not very dangerous for a man and his mother's brother's son to make love to the same girl if they are not members of the same local community. The most dangerous incest of this kind, the consequences of which 'split a man in two' with pain, is when father and son have relations with the same woman, for the father goes from the woman to the mother, thus bringing her into a sexual relationship with her son. It is also highly dangerous for a mother and daughter to have relations with the same man. In one village where I was living at the time relations of this kind were believed to have caused the death not only of the daughter but of her sister and half-sister as well. I knew of another case in which two sisters died after the same man had had relations with both of them. The man died shortly afterwards, and it was said that he had been summoned by the ghosts of the sisters.

There are, as we have seen, a very large number of relationships which carry the incest taboo and it is not surprising that there are frequent breaches of it. Indeed, Nuer discuss incest, except incest with the closest kin, without expressing horror or repugnance. It is a fact with which they are familiar and a subject on the surface of life, not a secret thing to be talked of with embarrassment. Parents teach sons at an early age the rules of sex: to avoid the wives of others and women who are kin. Not only must they refrain from making love to women who count as kin but they must avoid any licentious talk, to which the Nuer are much given, in their presence. The *nei ti gwagh*, the unrelated people, they can joke with and make love to without fear of censure or retribution, so long as they are not wives of other men, for fornication with an unrelated girl is not regarded with disapprobation. The admonition of parents is enforced by the frequent discussions children hear about the permissibility of proposed marriages and by the sacrifices on account of incest they are bound to witness from time to time.

The incest taboo is not uniform in its force nor in the consequences its breach is believed to entail. Some incest is very bad and has very serious consequences. Other incest is not so bad, is even thought little of, and is not expected to bring about serious, or even any, consequences. The worst incest of all would be with the mother, and Nuer were astonished when I asked them if they had known of any cases of it: 'But that would be immediate death.' Incest with the uterine sister or the daughter is also terrible. I have heard of one case of each. Incest with the paternal half-sister, whether daughter of pater or genitor, is bad but, so Nuer told me, occasionally occurs. Incest with cousins is not so bad and with paternal cousins not uncommon, 'for one man knows kinship and another man does not know kinship, that is a man whose heart was made differently'. Generally speaking, the farther the man and woman are from one another genealogically the less seriously incest between them is regarded, especially if they live in different districts, and the taboo is less stringent and has a narrower range for natural kinsmen than for legal kinsmen. I was told, for instance, that a man might make love to the daughter of a natural son of his maternal grandfather (*nya nar laka*). Incest with kinswomen on the paternal side is not thought so bad as incest with kinswomen on the maternal side. It is worse with the uterine sister than with the paternal half-sister, and it is worse with a mother's brother's daughter than with a father's brother's daughter, and with a mother's sister's daughter than with a father's sister's daughter. In all categories of incest it is considered much worse with a near kinswoman than a distant one. Relations with distant clanswomen and cognates are of frequent occurrence. They are with persons who are on the frontiers of prohibition and carry no moral stigma or much fear of consequences. Nuer, in the usual idiom of their culture, often condemn incest with kinsfolk by reference to bridewealth: 'Would you have relations with the daughter of your father's sister? Do you not receive cattle on her marriage?' Condemnation in such terms would not be applicable to distant kinsfolk.

Incest with wives of kinsmen also occurs, though I have little means of judging its frequency. I recorded two cases of incest with wives of maternal uncles. In the one the offender died of *rual*, while in the other the uncle, who was a rich man with several wives, sacrificed an ox and afterwards relinquished the wife in

11. A maiden, smoking pipe

favour of his sister's son: 'It was like making a gift to his sister's son.' I have also recorded cases of incest with another wife of the sister's husband. These cases come to light because the man or woman falls violently sick and to avoid death confesses what he or she has done and asks for an animal to be sacrificed in atonement. Intimacy with wives of paternal cousins and of other clansmen is undoubtedly common. As with incest with kinswomen, incest with wives of kinsmen is regarded in a more or less serious light according to the kinship distance separating the two men; likewise with relations between a woman and two kinsmen or between a man and two kinswomen. Thus in a village in Lou country where I was living it was common knowledge that a man called Lum was having an affair with a woman who was described to me as his wife's sister, and when I expressed astonishment that he should dare to continue it, I was told: 'It may be all right, she is only his wife's *nyagwanlen* (father's brother's daughter).' It remained to be seen whether there would be consequences or not. I was also told that even had the girl been his wife's *nyagwan* (paternal half-sister) nothing might happen, though the relations would without doubt be *rual*, and that the consequences would only be both certain and disastrous had she been his wife's *nyiman pany*, her true (uterine) sister.

Incest with the wife of a kinsman is also, of course, adultery, but if it is with the wife of a close kinsman who does not in this context count as a 'bull' the response is likely to emphasize the incest rather than the adultery. The husband, although he is the innocent party, may suffer harm, and if the incest comes to light he is anxious rather to have a sacrifice performed than to exact compensation. However, relations with wives of kinsmen seem generally to be with the wives of 'bulls', a man's paternal kin, who live in his village, and, as I have explained, they are not regarded as incestuous—neither are cattle demanded in compensation. Apart from the fact that their wives are all wives of the lineage, it is not thought proper that cattle should go from one kraal to another in payment for adultery among people who herd their cattle together and assist one another in debts. Thus, if a man commits adultery with his father's brother's wife he is not likely to be asked to pay more than 'the cow of the hide'. This animal, which is paid in addition to any cattle which may be paid in compensation for the wrong in any case of adultery, whether with the wife of a kinsman or with the wife of a stranger, is for sacrifice to prevent injury to the husband. It is not regarded as compensation for infringement of his rights.

More distant kinsmen are likely to insist on compensation. Relations with their wives are not thought to entail serious consequences on account of their incestuous nature, and there is less reason for the husband viewing the adultery with tolerance. Sometimes a kinsman accepts smaller compensation than an unrelated man would do. For example, in a case which came to my notice, a man had relations with the wife of the son of his maternal uncle's mother's sister. He paid three head of cattle in compensation, instead of the six head which might have been demanded, and he provided a goat for sacrifice. In all such cases, however, the outcome depends on the personal relations between the men concerned, and this generally means whether they are neighbours.

To avoid the consequences of incest Nuer make sacrifices, and the weight they attach to the breach of the taboo may be estimated by the value of the thing they sacrifice. For slight incest, as with a distant clanswoman or the wife of a paternal cousin, they consider it sufficient to sacrifice one of the yellow fruits I have spoken of earlier or one of the pendulous fruits of the sausage-tree. When a fruit is sacrificed it is cut in two and the left half, 'the bad half', is thrown away, while an infusion of the contents of the right half, 'the good half', is drunk by the partners to the sin. They may get a magician to make the sacrifice for them or they may make it for themselves. When incest has taken place with the wife of a kinsman who is not a 'bull' and is in Nuer reckoning a close kinsman, the wife's sleeping-skin is cut in two. This, of course, would only be done if one of the pair was sick enough to be more frightened of death than of the husband, for unlike the cutting of the fruits the rite cannot be performed secretly. In cases of incest with a close kinswoman and in all cases of what Nuer regard as really bad incest, *wal ruali*, an antidote some people are said to possess and make use of when committing a slight incest, is no protection and a vicarious sacrifice no remedy. A goat or a sheep, or in the most serious cases an ox, must be cut vertically in twain and a leopard-skin chief must perform the sacrifice. The guilty persons drink incest medicines infused in the gall of the sacrificed animal. It is believed that retribution follows swiftly on the heels of the offence, so that if sacrifice is to be of any avail it must be

performed at once. Nuer say that a sacrifice is unlikely to be effica-
cious when death is near and that it is little profit to make con-
fession then.

The presence of children increases the danger. It is not thought
that relations with a distant patrilineal cousin or with the wife of a
father's brother in the classificatory sense will harm those who
engage in them, but if the woman has children Nuer say: 'It (the
rual) may leave you alone, but it will kill the children.' In the same
way I was told in reference to the case, already cited, of Lum, who
was having relations with his wife and his wife's paternal cousin
at the same time: 'But she (the wife) has no child, so it is not *rual*.'
If she had had a child the paternal cousin would have been the ·
child's mother. In another case a man called Buk was having
relations with a concubine in a neighbouring hamlet although his
son, Bul, was married to the daughter of this concubine by another
man. It was stressed by informants that Buk had not begotten a
child by the concubine, for had he done so the child would have
been *gat gwan*, father's son, to Bul, whose marriage, which had in
any case not escaped critical comment, might then have entailed
risks. In Jikany country I recorded the following case. A man died
and his widow went to live with his brother. A third brother died
and there was talk of the living brother taking his widow also; but
he did not do so on the objection being raised that both widows
belonged to the same clan and that he had already begotten a child
by the first one. In another case, also in Jikany country, a man of
the Gaajak tribal area begat a child by his brother's widow, a
Gaatgankir clanswoman of the Gaajok tribal area. When he came
to live in the Gaajok tribal area he began affairs with two girls, but
gave them up when he found that they belonged to the widow's
clan, lest relations with them might injure his child. A man cannot
take as a concubine a woman who has borne a child in concubinage to one of his close kinsmen.

III

I now make some general observations on Nuer exogamous and
other marriage prohibitions and incest, or about the Nuer concept
of *rual*. Nuer say that marriage to persons standing in certain
relationships is forbidden because it would be *rual*, incestuous.
Speaking sociologically, I think we may reverse this statement and

say that sexual relations with persons standing in these relationships are considered incestuous because it would be a breach of the marriage prohibitions to marry them. I would hold that the incest taboo can only be understood by reference to the marriage prohibitions, and that these prohibitions must be viewed in the light of their function in the Nuer kinship system and in their whole social structure.

It is evident that the incest prohibition is derived from a social definition of kinship. There is no consanguinity between a man and his wife's sister, between an adopted Dinka boy and the daughter of his foster-father's brother, and between a man and the daughter of one of his age-mates. The Nuer incest prohibition is a prohibition of sexual relations within relationships of certain kinds, and I suggest that its range of extension may be related to the marriage prohibitions of their society for which it provides a moral norm, a reason, and a sanction.

It is true that extra-marital relations between clansfolk who do not belong to the same lineage do not occasion great concern, but I do not think that this invalidates the contention, for though they take place they are none the less *rual* and the toleration of the breach of the taboo merely means, as it does in other cases in which a breach is tolerated, that the nearer we get to the point at which marriage is permitted the less stringent becomes the prohibition of sexual relations. It must also be remembered that agnation is recognized beyond the clan and between clans, and that the Nuer themselves recognize that the limits of exogamy are fixed arbitrarily. That sexual relations with distant clanswomen are little condemned shows that we are dealing with a prohibition the strength of which is relative to the structural positions of the persons concerned, just as is the force of customary law, and that the prohibition of marriage is more fundamental and comprehensive than the prohibition of sex relations, which is secondary and, I would hold, derivative. That it is the table of prohibited degrees and not the incest taboo which is basic is further illustrated by the prohibition, at the present day a qualified prohibition, on marriage with the daughter of a father's age-mate, for sexual relations between men and women standing in this relationship to one another are entirely free from any stigma and if either father is dead marriage may take place.

It is also true that Nuer call *rual* relations with women married to kinsmen. These women cannot be counted as possible mates to whom any marriage prohibitions could apply. But it must be pointed out that Nuer bring wives of kinsmen within the field of kinship values, not only in that they address them by kinship terms, but also, and more significantly, by reference to their children, for according to Nuer ideas marriage is only a complete union when a child has been born of it. Mothers through their children become kinsfolk and are thus brought within the circuit of the incest taboo not so much as wives of kinsmen but rather as mothers of kinsmen.

In view of the importance attached to children by Nuer in determining what is incest, or the degree of it, it may readily be understood why sexual relations with the wives of half-brothers, paternal uncles, and patrilineal cousins of every degree are regarded as being either incestuous peccadillos or not incestuous at all. The wife of a 'bull' is, in a general social sense, the wife of all the 'bulls', of the paternal kin, and of the lineage. She is 'our wife' and 'the wife of our cattle'. Likewise her children are the children of the lineage, of the agnatic group, and of its cattle. Hence sexual relations with wives of these agnates, if not approved, are condoned, for they are the wives of all. Hence, also, whereas relations with, for example, the wife of the maternal uncle means relations with the *cek nara*, the maternal uncle's wife, and the mother of *gat nara*, the maternal uncle's child, relations with the wife of the father's brother's son are with '*cekdan*', 'our wife', and the mother of '*gatdan*', 'our child'. The presence of a child does not alter the status of the persons concerned in the second case as it does in the first, for the wife is the wife of the lineage and the child is the child of the adulterer. When a man dies, therefore, there is no question of the widow being remarried to one of his brothers, for the brothers already count as her husbands. The dead man's lineage have a right to inherit his wife because she is their wife, the wife of their cattle.

I think that we should try to interpret in much the same way the feeling that it is wrong for two kinsmen to court the same girl, unless they are members of the same lineage. Paternal kin can share the same girl because they have a lineage identity, whereas the courting of the same girl by, for example, a man and his maternal aunt's son makes for confusion within the kinship system. The position of the uterine brother is peculiar because full brothers are not just 'bulls' to one another, members of the same lineage. They are maternal kinsmen as well as paternal kinsmen, and in their case sexual relations with each other's sweethearts seem to the Nuer to involve in some way the mother, an idea which is repugnant to them.

These interpretations may be unacceptable to the reader. If so, he can disregard them without rejecting the main conclusion from which they are inferred. It is clear that the marriage prohibitions indicate kinship status and are one of the most effective means of doing this and thereby maintaining the kinship system, which is based on the distinctions between the various categories of relationships. They prevent confusion between one relationship and another and the contradictions such confusion would cause between the patterns of behaviour in which the relationships are expressed. This conclusion is contained in the statements, some of them recorded in this chapter, of Nuer themselves, who see that it is undesirable to obliterate or obscure the boundaries between kinship categories. Were marriage with the wife's sister permitted, to the child of it the mother's sister would also be the father's wife; and were a man to marry the daughter of an age-mate, his age-mate would also be his father-in-law.

The bearing these regulations have on the kinship system will be seen in later chapters. I discussed their bearing on political structure and their relation to the lineage system in a few pages (pp. 225–8) in *The Nuer*. The argument there presented may be restated in a few sentences. Nuer political structure is a system of relations between territorial groups which express both their autonomy and their participation in the system in terms of lineage and clan affiliations. The local groups are organized into a common tribal structure through the association of clans with tribes, and the various lineages of these dominant clans in each tribe with the various sections and sub-sections of the tribe. Political structure is thus conceptualized in lineage structure. To play this part lineages must be both unique groups and at the same time must be identified with the local communities within which they function politically. Were they to lose entirely their uniqueness as descent groups the lineage structure in which the local communities see themselves as parts of a tribal organization would collapse. Were they not to merge in the network of kinship relations of which each local community is composed they would lack that corporateness which identification with residential groups gives them, and be an abstraction, since they are not corporate groups in their own right. A man acts sometimes as a lineage member, cutting himself off from the community of which he is part, but in ordinary social life he acts as a member of this community without reference to his exclusive lineage affiliation. In some situations values of descent determine his conduct, but in most situations it is determined by kinship values or by those community values which are an expression on a political plane of a sentiment created by corporate life comprised within a network of personal relations of a kinship order. This separation of the lineage from community life and its merging into it again is very largely brought about by the rules of exogamy which exclude marriage within the clan, thus giving that group distinctness, while compelling its lineages, by marrying outside the clan, to become multiple links in the network of kinship relations the strands of which form the texture of community life. Every Nuer local community thus becomes a community of kin, every member of which regulates his behaviour to every other member in accordance with a variety of kinship patterns and can predict their behaviour to himself in conformity with the same norms.

When a local community becomes in this way a network of kinship ties it is necessary, so varied and extensive are the relationships which come under the ban on marriage, to marry outside it, so that not only is the social autonomy of lineage groups prevented by the rules regulating marriage but also the social autonomy of residential groups. Kinship ties thus cross the gaps in political structure and unite members of opposed segments of it. Every political group of whatever size has a wider social setting outside its boundaries.

There is a tendency therefore for local communities to be groups of people who, being all interrelated in one way or another, must marry into a different local community. This happens because the Nuer make any kind of cognatic relationship to several degrees a bar to marriage and, at least so it seems to me, it is a bar to marriage because of the fundamental agnatic principle running through Nuer society. In any Nuer residential group, of whatever size, there is, as we have seen, a great variety of personal ties of a kinship order bringing its members into a texture of relationships, but the warp of the texture is the agnatic lineage and to it everyone attaches himself locally. If a man is not a member of the lineage with which he lives, he makes himself a member of it by treating a maternal link as though it was a paternal one or through affinal relationship. The lineage is thus in its corporate character a composite structure of cognatic branches and attachments in which the value of agnation is the integrating principle. The solidarity of a group of persons living together, and thereby the lineage structure which contains them, is maintained by emphasizing cognation in the rules of exogamy.

III. A youth. His hair is dressed with ashes

CHAPTER III

MARRIAGE

I

I HAVE suggested in the last chapter that the range of the Nuer incest taboo can be understood only in relation to their rules prohibiting marriage between kin. These in their turn are only intelligible when viewed as part of the kinship system to which they belong, and that kinship system derives its particular form from its function in the political structure of the Nuer.

Kinship is a general word for describing any relationship of one individual to another through his father or mother. All kinship ties thus derive from the family, that universal and fundamental social group which everywhere and in some way or another incorporates the institution of marriage. It is therefore partly for logical reasons that I describe first how matrimonial unions are brought about among the Nuer and discuss the kinship relations which derive from them later. I describe marriage and kinship in this order also partly for convenience, in that kinship among the Nuer is so largely defined by reference to bridewealth.

I describe in this first section relations between the sexes before marriage, and in the following sections the chief ceremonies by which marriage is brought about, the payments of bridewealth which together with the ceremonies create valid and durable unions, the affinal relations which arise from the unions, and the various forms of domestic union we find among the Nuer side by side with matrimony in the full legal sense.

Sexual activities are from their earliest manifestations given the stamp of cultural values. They are from the first associated with marriage, which is the final goal of the sex life of men and women. Even the very poor and the disabled form domestic establishments of some kind and talk proudly of 'my father-in-law' and 'my mother-in-law'. It is the chief ambition of a youth to marry and have a home (*gol*) of his own, for when Nuer speak of marriage they speak of a home. They say of a youth: 'He is married—he has a *gol*.' Even in childhood it is clear to Nuer that marriage and the birth of children are the ultimate purpose of the sexual functions to which all earlier activities of a sexual kind—play, love-making, and courtship—are a prelude, a preparation, and a means.

So long as there is no erotic behaviour in public, no inhibitions attach to sexual interests and their expression, and no one tries to hide from children the facts of sexual life, which they can learn by observing their elders and the flocks and herds among which childhood is spent. A boy who is seen by his elders in sexual play with a girl of his own age will merely be told not to act as though he had been initiated—he can do what he likes then—and at the most might receive a cut with a grass switch. No one considers his conduct immoral, and the older people will joke about such things among themselves.

Children start playing at marriage from the time they begin to walk, at first as uncomprehending observers of the games of older children and then as participants in 'them. They make cattle byres and huts of sand, and mud oxen and cows, and with these conduct bridewealth negotiations and perform marriage ceremonies, and they play at domestic and conjugal life, including sometimes in the game, I was told, imitation of coitus. In its earliest expression, therefore, sex is associated with marriage, and the first sexual play occurs in imitation of one of the domestic routines of married life. It occurs in response to a cultural, and not to an instinctive, urge.

Girls and boys, the girls rather earlier than the boys, begin to perform the simpler and lighter tasks of household and kraal from about the age of seven. From then onwards till they are about fourteen, marriage games continue when the children are by themselves, and though within them sexual play begins to be indulged in for its own sake and not merely in imitation of adult behaviour, it is subordinate to the whole make-believe relationship of conjugality of which it forms a part. During the rainy months the girls visit the boys in the grazing grounds, bringing them balls of porridge as presents, which each gives to the boy she has chosen as her 'husband'. She also milks the goats for her 'husband' and may even bring him a gourdful of cow's milk from the kraal. The boys cut millet stalks in the gardens and after roasting and eating the immature grain send the sweet stalks with their outer husks removed to their 'brides'. Older boys also send their juniors with mud oxen and cows to one of the senior girls, who plays the part of mother-in-law. I was told that in these games sexual intercourse may take place, but is neither a usual nor a prominent feature.

Girls witness serious love-making and courtship earlier than boys. At dances small girls follow their more experienced sisters and cousins, imitating their movements during the dancing and afterwards sitting with them while the young men pay them compliments and try to persuade them to retire with them into the long grass. When a girl is about twelve or thirteen initiated boys begin to court her, and when she is about fifteen or sixteen she has at least one lover and probably one in each of the villages neighbouring her own. She passes through a succession of love affairs, besides more casual affairs. I doubt whether any girl in Nuerland goes to her husband a virgin.

As a rule boys are initiated from about fourteen to sixteen. Unlike the girls, whose social life develops slowly from childhood to marriage without any sudden change of status, the boys jump at initiation from the grade of boyhood to the grade of manhood, and the character of their social life is correspondingly transformed; though even before initiation boys make some adjustments in their way of life in anticipation of the status they will acquire when they have passed through the rites. In particular, they abstain from eating in the presence of unrelated girls. A small boy eats with his mother and sisters, but when he is about six he eats with the other boys of the household when the womenfolk have guests, lest they might feel embarrassed at the presence of a lad, though only a small one, and, bit by bit, he gets into the habit of eating with them regularly.

After initiation a lad takes on the full privileges and obligations of manhood in work, play, and war. Above all, he gives himself whole-heartedly to winning the favours of the maidens of his neighbourhood. Courtship now rivals devotion to cattle as his major interest. In speaking of a recently initiated lad Nuer often say: 'And now he has become a man and will court the girls.' He takes every opportunity for flirtation which offers itself. His chances are chiefly at dances, and Nuer youths, for this reason, attend as many wedding dances and other drum-dances as they can in their district during the rains and the harp-dances at neighbouring camps in the dry season. In speaking of these dances young men speak always of the girls they will meet at them, of how the girls will admire their finery and their excellent dancing and display of spearmanship and duelling with the club, and they add: 'And then of course we will spend the night in courting.'

That Nuer do not attend dances chiefly for the dancing is shown by their lack of interest in organizing harp-dances in dry-season camps when it is unlikely that unrelated girls from other camps will be able to attend them. 'Who wants to dance with his sisters?' they ask. But when there is a chance of love-making Nuer youths, who appear so slothful and lethargic to the foreign traveller, think nothing of walking and running ten to fifteen miles to attend a dance.

When a dance breaks up, about nine o'clock at night, the youths seize the girls by their wrists and lead them apart. They then either walk about the dancing-ground in pairs and small groups, the youths and maidens hand-in-hand or with their arms round each other's waists, or they sit in small parties at the grass-fringed edge of the dancing-ground. They sit wedged together and exchange endearments. Nuer girls are attractive companions at any time and are enchanting when decked with flowers and ornaments and anointed with oil for dancing, and the young men are charming and indefatigable flatterers. Wooing in Nuerland is an arduous business. A youth must be profuse and tireless in pouring out compliments to the girl whose favour he solicits, and he often sits opposite her with a stick in his hand to make lines on the ground to mark each new compliment.

When these parties break up the youths and maidens pair and continue flirting *tête-a-tête* in the grasses in privacy. It rests entirely with a girl whom she goes with. She has her lovers who meet her whenever they can, at dances, at her father's home, and at trysting-places, and she will probably go with one of these. When several young men want to go with her they tell her to make her choice from them, for all those who have been sitting together with the girl belong to one *dep*, the fighting line of a village, and are therefore all kin who will not quarrel about a girl. A lover from a different village would not try to break into the circle once it has been formed. She makes her choice—if she already has a lover in the *dep* she will choose him—and the other youths move away. Apart from her established lovers, a girl has no difficulty in knowing if a man is particularly attracted to her by the way he dances and conducts his spear-thrusting and club-duelling exercises during the dancing. If she likes him also she can probably so arrange matters that he is able to seize her wrist when the dance is beginning to break up.

Intercourse does not necessarily take place when a youth and maid are alone together on the night of a dance. When the relationship between them is a *luom buol,* a dance love affair, or *luom thura,* a dancing-ground love affair, a more or less constant attachment, and not a *luom goka,* a love affair of the high grasses, casual lust, I was told that the girl is likely to refuse her favours, though he will entreat for them, unless she feels sure that he intends to marry her and has the cattle with which to do so, for no respectable girl wants to be a *keagh,* an unmarried mother. No attempt is made to conceal an attachment of this kind, which indeed imposes on the girl modesty and shyness towards her lover in the presence of other persons such as a bride is expected to show towards her bridegroom or a newly-wed towards her husband.

Parents are not cognizant of all the love affairs of their children, but if a girl forms a constant attachment she may tell her mother about it, and a father will probably hear of a similar attachment of his son. They are not likely to say anything unless there is danger of incest. All the young men of a hamlet or small village, who are kinsmen and dance together, know of one another's court-ships and escapades. Likewise, all the girls know about one another's lovers and amours, for they also keep together at dances. The only person who may interfere is a brother in an affair of his sister, for her virtue is his responsibility, but he will only do so in certain circumstances. He keeps an eye on his sister and knows who is courting her, but he will only come between her and her lover if he suspects that she is having regular relations with a man without cattle or that she is giving herself to all and sundry.

It not infrequently happens that a girl becomes pregnant while still unmarried. If the young man has cattle he will be expected to marry her, and if she is not a profligate he will be glad to do so. If he has insufficient cattle he cannot do so, and though another man will not object to taking her as a wife, he is more likely to take her as a second wife than as a first wife, and he will pay fewer cattle for her bridewealth. It is therefore in the brother's interest to see that this does not happen. It is also in his interest to prevent his sister from becoming a wanton. A man does not expect his bride to be a virgin, but he does not care to marry a jade. A girl of easy virtue may find plenty of lovers but no suitors, and after bearing an illegitimate child is likely to become a concubine for the rest of her life, to the detriment of her family herd.

Therefore, if a youth takes a girl away from a dance to his *dep* and sits with her among his friends and other girls until he finds an opportunity to get her to himself he will not be molested, because her brother has seen her leave the dance in company, and by the time she is intimate with her lover he will be doing the same himself. But if a man is indiscreet enough to take her off by herself as soon as the dance is breaking up he is asking for trouble, though the brother may not say anything if the youth is a friend of his whom he knows to have cattle and serious intentions towards his sister. If the young man is a casual lover he may tap him on the shoulder with the butt of his spear, when he will run away; or even fight him. However, there need be no trouble if the conventions are observed.

Courtship seems to be freest among the Eastern Jikany. There love affairs are carried on more or less openly, and a youth need not fear the girl's brother so long as they are on friendly terms and he is discreet. The girls of this area are, however, said to be less free with their favours than those of the Lou tribe. They are exacting in their demands for fine speeches, but will not allow intimacy unless they are sure that pregnancy will be followed by marriage. The Lou girls are said to be easier and their brothers more difficult. To the west of the Nile, at any rate in some parts, it is said that a girl's brother has the right to take a male calf and a cow calf if he catches a man having relations with his sister, but this penalty seems only to be exacted when it is believed that pregnancy has ensued, and I was told that if the beasts have been seized they will be returned should it be found that she had not conceived. If she is pregnant, they will be kept pending marriage negotiations.

A youth may have several sweethearts in different villages and a girl several lovers in different villages. At this time of his life a young man models himself on the accepted pattern of what a young man should be to win the approbation of his sweethearts and the regard of girls generally. He likes to know that they are looking at him and saying about him, when they chat together and share their secrets, that he is a *wut pany*, a real man. He pays great attention to his appearance and takes every opportunity to excel in feats of endurance and courage. It is for the benefit of the girls that he leaps behind his oxen in dry-season camps, 'when the people have met together', and chants poems. When asked whether a man would chant if there were no girls near, a Nuer replied: 'And if there were no girls near, what would he chant for?' A youth who wants a girl in marriage goes to her village or camp in the evening and chants there for an hour or two. He knows that she will understand that the poem is about herself. Her relatives know why he has come.

A youth is particularly careful not to be seen eating by unrelated girls: 'If he is not making love to them, he may do so some time or to one of their relatives.' When I asked whether it would matter if your sisters saw you eating, the reply was, 'Do you make love to your sisters?' Food must never be mentioned in the presence of girls, and a man will endure severe hunger rather than let them know that he has not eaten for a long time. It is a strict rule of Nuer society that the sexes, unless they are close kin, avoid each other in the matter of food. Nuer do not go near persons of the other sex when they are eating. A man may mention food but not sexual matters before kinswomen, and he may mention sexual matters but not food before unrelated girls.

Girls are the arbiters of decorum, and the severest sanction of a breach of good form is their disapproval. Not only is the shame of it a sanction for etiquette, but it is a powerful influence in making a youth generous, respectful to his elders, dutiful to his parents and kinsmen, hospitable to guests, industrious, and brave. The girls on their side are anxious to earn the good opinion of youths by correct behaviour in the home and in society.

It will have been observed that it rests entirely with a girl whether she accepts a man's attentions and how far he presses his advances. A girl who is fond of a youth wants him to marry her. If he is philandering she will, if she has any regard for her chastity, be frugal with her favours. The talk between a youth and his sweetheart is frequently the topic of marriage. He asks her whether she will marry him, and she says that she will if he has cattle and her parents consent; or he entreats her to allow intimacy, and she urges that she might become pregnant and he not marry her, and she would then be in trouble. However, if a girl is in love with a youth, and he has a winning manner, she may surrender to his pleading. Men often break the promises they make to girls when they want favours from them, and in looking for a wife a man may pass over all his sweethearts, past and present, and go with his friends to seek a spouse outside the circle of his usual acquaintances.

One reason why this sometimes happens is that a man's sweethearts are frequently of his own age and Nuer usually marry girls younger than themselves. The prohibition on marriage to the daughter of a father's age-mate also influences a man's choice of a wife. Nevertheless, it is probably more usual for a man to choose one of his sweethearts. Marriage is the purpose implicit in every romance.

Sometimes a girl herself makes a proposal of marriage. She goes with some companions of her sex to the kraal of her favourite and drives away several of his father's cows to her home. Her father knows what she wants when he sees her returning with the cows, and if he disapproves of the youth he will send them back. If he likes the young man he says nothing, and when several days have passed and the cattle have not been returned, the young man knows that the girl's people are willing to discuss the matter. A father does not care to refuse his daughter when she is very much in love with a man, even when he is not rich, in case she runs away from home or hangs herself. Another way in which a girl can make a public proposal of marriage is a custom of early dry-season camps. Youths of a camp take their favourite oxen to parade them, led by their younger brothers, round a neighbouring camp, while they chant poems behind them and make graceful leaps into the air (*rau*). A girl who loves a youth may on such an occasion seize his ox and remove its lead. By so doing she pledges the youths to return to a harp-dance on another day. She keeps the cord and attaches a metal ring to it. Its owner later sends a small brother to fetch it. This is tantamount to a proposal and acceptance of marriage, and if the young man has enough cattle the betrothal ceremony takes place soon afterwards.

The facts outlined in this section lead to two conclusions: that there is wide sexual freedom before marriage, and that sex life is from the beginning stamped by cultural interests. Apart from rules of incest, adultery, and good form, there are no checks placed on the expression of sex from its earliest manifestations. Nevertheless, even at the outset the compass is set towards marriage and children. Simulated coitus between children is part of a game of domestic and marital relationships. After initiation, young men make love to girls as much as they can, but though there is much casual intercourse it is considered rather gross, and the aim of both youths and girls is to form attachments of the lover-sweetheart kind, in which coitus, when it takes place at all, is only part of a more complex relationship. The lover-sweetheart relationship has within it the purpose or pretence of marriage. Very likely a particular courtship will not develop into marriage, but courtship is the recognized prelude to matrimony, and if a youth wants favours from his sweetheart, he must persuade her of his intentions. A love affair tends, therefore, to be a marriage courtship, and for this reason the pattern of the husband-wife relationship in the first stage of married life intrudes into it, and the pair act towards one another with the conjugal reserve of this stage. So strong is the cultural idea of marriage that, though devoid of irksome restraint and inhibitions, the path of sex life runs from childhood towards that union and, though circuitous, leads always to wedding, home, and family. Marriage is the end of a full sex life. After he is married a man settles down to care of herds and gardens, and goes less and less to dances, and ceases to take much interest in girls. I was told that should he wish to have an affair with a girl his wife would have no objection and would probably help him in it. Women, on the other hand, once they are married, ought not to have relations with men other than their husbands.

Men now expect to marry younger than in the last generation, when, I was told, a man would not usually marry before he was 25 to 30. Fathers were wont to say that they would themselves marry again, for these young wives would in any case go to their sons when they were dead. At what age a youth marries today depends on the size of his family, his place in it, whether his father is dead, the size of his family herd, and other circumstances.

As a rule, girls marry round about 17 or 18, though one sometimes sees an unmarried girl of over 20. If a girl is betrothed early the wedding and consummation ceremonies are delayed. Women, therefore, have their first children at an age when they are well fitted to bear them. So long as a girl is married to a man with cattle she has fairly free choice of a mate. Much depends on whether the girl's family approve of the man's family. In theory, the parents choose their daughter's husband and only formally ask her consent, which she should give in duty to her parents, for marriage is not her business but the business of her menfolk. In fact, it is very difficult for parents to force their daughter to marry a man she dislikes, and strong-minded girls stand up against family pressure on this issue.

In general, therefore, it may be said that if there is no kinship between a youth and a maiden and the youth's father has sufficent cattle, marriage is unlikely to be opposed by either family, unless there is bad blood between them. The first condition, however, makes it difficult usually for a man to find a mate in his own village, since, as we have seen, villagers are generally in one way or another kin. Also, a man is unlikely, except in parts of western Nuerland where some of the tribes are very small and there is much intercommunication between tribe and tribe, to marry outside his tribe, unless he lives near its border with another tribe, for he may then have relatives and friends on the other side of the border with whom he visits and on whom he can rely for help should difficulties arise about the return of his cattle in the event of divorce. Hence a man may generally be expected—I cannot give figures for the distribution of marriages—to take a wife from some village of his own tribe and within easy reach of his own village, that is to say, within his district or from among the people whom he habitually visits.

This fact, combined with the frequency with which Nuer live with their affines and maternal kin and their wandering and migratory tendencies, has produced a very great admixture within local groups of persons belonging to diverse lineages and tribal and foreign origins. It means also that, as I have already explained, any Nuer has kinship links of one kind or another with persons belonging to many different local communities. With each marriage these strands running from one community to another are increased and there results a complex network of kinship ties between members of opposed segments within the political structure.

II

Marriage among the Nuer is brought about by payment of bridewealth and by the performance of certain ceremonial rites. The rites cannot take place without the payments, but transfers of cattle do not by themselves bring about the union. Both are necessary, and they proceed in a connected movement towards the full establishment of the union. Each enforces and reinforces the other. The bride's people can, by holding up the rites, put pressure on the bridegroom's people to make the payments due to them,

and the bridegroom's people can, by withholding the cattle, in-
duce the girl's family and kin to advance the ceremonies. First one
pedal is pressed down and then the other as the marriage is pro-
pelled to its appointed end, the birth of children and the sharing
of a home. It is understood that payments should have reached a
certain point before a certain rite is held, and the performance of
the rite is a recognition of the transfer of cattle up to that point.
Payments of cattle and marriage rites therefore tend to alternate,
though there is no fixity about the alternation and no marriage is
exactly the same as another in this respect. The new social ties of
conjugality and affinity are made stronger by each payment and
by each ceremony, so that a marriage which is insecure at the
beginning of the negotiations becomes surer with every new payment and rite; both sides, by the giving and receiving of cattle and
by joint participation in the rites, becoming more deeply committed to bringing about the union. Therefore a marriage which
has reached the final rites may be regarded as a stable union and
will generally prove to be so.

The chief ceremonies are the *larcieng*, the *ngut*, and the *mut*:
the betrothal, the wedding, and the consummation. All three are
important public events in Nuer life, though the betrothal rites
are not held on so large a scale to the west of the Nile as to the east.
Preparations for them are made days, even weeks, ahead, and they
are talked about, especially by the young people, long before they
take place. They are usually held in the rains, for there is then
plenty of millet for porridge and beer, and people have the energy
of the well-fed and can travel long distances without fatigue and
dance and make love with equal vigour. A whole district attends
them, the mere coming together of so many people making
marriage a memorable event. Neighbours thus bear witness to the
creation of the new social ties and by their presence sanction them.

Neighbours form the crowd at marriage feasts. They have no
direct concern with the union. Apart from these people who
attend the ceremonies for dancing and flirting and for the general
sociability and excitement, are those who attend them for more
serious purposes. It will be seen that there are always, besides pro-
longed discussions about bridewealth, sacrifices and other rites
which have to be performed and which interest only some of the
people present—the families and kin of the bride and bridegroom.
These are the rites which express the relations between husband

and wife, husband's kin and wife's kin, and between the kin on one side or the other and the ghosts and spirits of their lineage. Those who stand outside these relationships are only spectators and often pay no attention to the rites at all. It is the dance which gives to the ceremonies their popularity and publicity; it is the rites which express and bring about their purpose.

Generally, as we have seen, there has long been an understanding between the youth and the girl he wishes to marry and she has been his sweetheart, though sometimes a youth decks himself as a bridegroom and in the company of another youth, arrayed in the ornaments of a best man, tours the country-side in search of a bride. In either case, the youth does not ask for the hand of the girl without her consent. He and his friends must then ask her family and they consult their kinsfolk. They know what is going on long before they are formally asked for her hand, so when a girl tells her menfolk in the byre that there are guests outside who wish to speak to them, the men know what they have come for. The suitor and his friends enter the byre and seat themselves to the right, the girl's people being seated to the left. They say that the girl has accepted them and ask whether the elders will accept them also. The elders ask them what cattle they have. This is the *riet ghok*, the cattle talk. The best man answers for the suitor, who, to create a good impression, says as little as possible. Both wear skins to cover their genitals before possible future parents-in-law. The bridegroom's best man and two other friends accompany him through all the trials of marriage and take full advantage of the opportunities for love-making and courtship. The girl's people accept the suit in a preliminary way and the youths depart to eat at a neighbouring homestead, since the suitor cannot eat in the home of the bride even at this stage.

There will later be other and more formal and definite discussions about the cattle in the byre of the father of the girl. The suitor has in the meanwhile been able to consult his own family and kinsmen, and when he returns with his friends for further talks the cattle are more precisely specified and ear-marked for particular claimants. The girl's people are satisfied. They say that the marriage is finished and tell the bridegroom, as he can now properly be called, and his friends to bring the *ghok lipa*, the cattle of betrothal, on a certain day. The discussions are still in an early stage, and by 'finished' they mean only that they are prepared to continue negotiations on the basis of the demands already met and to hold the betrothal ceremony. Before the visitors rise to go various men who can claim distant cognatic kinship with the bride, too distant for them to receive assigned portions of the bridewealth, may ask for gifts, ranging from a 'cow' (which means a sheep or goat) to a spear. Some of their demands are at once satisfied, the spears being handed over there and then, while others are met with promises or evasions.

A betrothal ceremony is not necessary. It is possible to proceed at once to the full wedding ceremony, and this is sometimes done when the bridegroom is a rich man with plenty of cattle and the bride is a *jut*, a girl who has passed the usual age of marriage. Usually the betrothal ceremony is held in the rainy season and the wedding in the following windy season. If there is a longer interval it is generally due to the immaturity of the bride. A poor suitor may pay two or three cows to a man who is short of stock at the time in order to obtain a lien on his small daughter while he collects adequate bridewealth to marry her later. Were the suitor a richer man he would seek a bride among older maidens, and were the father a richer man he would not feel the need to betroth his daughter at so early an age. A nubile maiden would not be betrothed for several years to a poor man. Her brothers would not brook the delay, for they themselves want to marry with the cattle of her bridewealth. Moreover, she would almost certainly become pregnant by some lover.

The holding of the betrothal ceremony means that the marriage is provisionally agreed upon by both sides, and the transfer to the bride's family of the cattle of the betrothal, three or four to ten head, is a further acknowledgement of this understanding. Before the ceremony takes place it has been agreed upon in general terms how many cattle should eventually be handed over. The ceremony is held in the bride's home. When the morning work of the kraal is finished the bridegroom and his party drive before them the cattle of the betrothal, led by a fine ox, the pride of the herd, its horns decorated with tassels, for the bride's brother. They advance on the bride's village in war formation and continue their marital exercises in her father's kraal, chanting their war songs before the huts and byres, especially before the hut of the bride's mother, who must be shown particular respect. The bridegroom's girl relatives and friends arrive about the same time as the men and they also dance in the kraal. The youths of the bride's village then form their *dep*, village fighting formation, and start their own exercises and the girls of the village their dancing. Then the drums are brought out and general dancing begins. Towards sunset the betrothal cattle, which were left outside the village to graze, are brought into the kraal and tethered. Dancing, duelling, singing, and love-making between the youths and maidens continue well into the night, and all pay special attention to the bridegroom, resplendent with his ivory armlets and his tight-fitting armlet of brass rings, and distinguished also by the wedding stick in his hand. Before midnight the father of the bride leads forth an ox which, with a ceremonial rubbing of ashes on its back, is dedicated to the lineage ghosts and spirits in a long address by the *gwan buthni*, a man of a collateral lineage who acts for his family on ceremonial occasions as master of ceremonies. He tells the spirits to take their ox and let the people be at peace. His address is followed by shorter speeches by old men of the bride's kin and perhaps by her father, all first rubbing ashes on the beast's back. The *jicoa*, the bridegroom's people, take no part in these proceedings, but the flesh of the sacrifice is, with the exception of head, neck, and some of the entrails, their right, and if the ox is not to their liking they insist on a bigger one being sacrificed or, which amounts to the same thing from their point of view, being slaughtered for their dinner. When the addresses are finished the master of ceremonies of the bride's lineage, or her father or another of her senior kinsmen, stabs the ox to the heart with a single thrust. It stands for a moment and falls to the ground, those present watching to see if it falls cleanly. The bridegroom's people, often directed by the bridegroom, though he may not himself eat in the home of his future father-in-law, amid much shouting and chaffing, divide the meat among themselves, each kinsman receiving his customary due. The ribs and part of the back are taken next day by the visiting girls to their parents and elders in the bridegroom's village and the rest is eaten on the spot. The girls of the bride's village who, like its menfolk, receive little or none of the meat, are up half the night cooking porridge, preparing beer, and boiling the meat for their guests, for the girls of the bridegroom's party are too busy flirting with the youths to assist them.

In the morning there is more dancing and beer is served to the guests before they depart. Shortly before they go, the bridegroom, if he has not done so earlier, throws on to the threshold of his mother-in-law's hut, if she has not yet reached the menopause, a tethering-cord, as an earnest that the *yang pal*, a cow to prolong her fertility, will be paid. He will already have given her a present of tobacco.

The wedding takes place some weeks later, and in the meanwhile there are further discussions about bridewealth not only in the home of the bride's father but also in the home of her senior maternal uncle, who is responsible for the negotiations on the mother's side. His claims are less flexible and there cannot be much dispute about them, so it sometimes happens that they are settled provisionally in the father's byre, and that the final discussions with the uncle himself, who may live far away, are left till after the wedding or even till after the consummation. Some more cattle will probably be handed over before the wedding.

Between the betrothal and the wedding the bridegroom is *lipe nyal*, a man to whom a bride is affianced, but he and she are spoken of as man and wife and the bridegroom acts towards his in-laws with the full respect due from a son-in-law. From time to time he visits his bride's home in the company of his best man and other friends, and on these occasions he may try to have relations with her, but it will be difficult for him because he is closely watched and others probably share the hut in which he and she are sleeping. In any case he cannot enforce marital rights at this stage, and his only hope is to get his best man to persuade his bride to visit him in the gardens.

Both sides want to complete the marriage without undue delay. The bridegroom's people want their wife and the bride's people want their cattle so that they themselves can marry. They do not care to use the cattle of the betrothal for this purpose because these are only on pledge and, if negotiations break down, have at once to be returned, or others substituted if they have died. In the interval between betrothal and wedding ceremonies a penultimate agreement is reached about the cattle and both parties have had time to accommodate themselves to their new interrelationships. Neither party would pursue the marriage to the point of holding the wedding, with its expense and publicity, unless they were confident of the outcome.

Arrangements are made to hold the wedding on a certain day. In the homestead of the bride the reception, especially the beer, is being prepared, and in the homestead of the bridegroom there is much rejoicing, men and women chanting poems into the night. They also chant on their way to the wedding and during its celebration. The main features of a wedding are discussion about cattle in the morning and the invocation over the cattle of the bridewealth (*twoc ghok*), the wedding dance, and the wedding sacrifice, in the afternoon and evening.

Early in the morning the bridegroom's kin discuss the situation in his father's byre. They know what outstanding claims are likely to be advanced because they know the persons on the other side who stand in those relationships to the bride to which beasts are due by custom. They run over their herds and assign particular beasts to meet probable claims, so that no last-moment demand shall be made which they have not allowed for and cannot reject. Similar talks are going on among the bride's kin in her father's byre. They know more or less what animals the bridegroom can muster, and they have also to agree on the division of the bridewealth among themselves; the problem often being not so much the total number of beasts to be paid but to which of the bride's kin they shall be allotted. The bride's father will do his best to protect his son-in-law against too greedy kinsmen. As we have seen, the bridegroom's people have several times discussed the whole question of the bridewealth with the bride's people, but there are certain demands not yet agreed to, or kept back till the last moment so that they can be exacted under threat of forbidding the wedding dance.

The older people of the bridegroom's kin go ahead of the bridegroom's party of youths and maidens to the bride's home to finish the discussions in the late morning and early afternoon. They are generally still arguing when the bridegroom's party arrives, the paternal uncles on both sides taking the foremost part, for it is thought impolite of the fathers to take too prominent a part in the discussions, especially if they are younger than the uncles. The bridegroom's kin sit on the right side of the byre and the bride's kin on the left side, as they would sit were a case being arbitrated between them by a leopard-skin chief. The byre has been swept clean in expectation of the guests, and ox-hides and mats have been spread on the floor. The bridegroom and his master of ceremonies and the bride's father and his master of ceremonies wear wild-cat skins round their loins to hide their nakedness, and

the master of ceremonies of the bridegroom holds a wedding stick
across his knees. After the involved Nuer greetings have been
exchanged they begin the final cattle talk over their pipes, each
claim being stated and restated and discussed in the deliberate
Nuer way—puff, puff, puff of tobacco, a few words, then puff, puff,
puff again. While the *jicuong*, the people with rights to cattle of
the bridewealth, are developing their claims, first on the father's
side, then on the mother's side, the master of ceremonies of the
bride brings a tray on which are lumps of tobacco and an equal
number of pieces of charcoal and hands these round to the bridegroom's senior relatives. The cattle talk, even at this stage, is often
loud and it looks, till one is used to Nuer, as though agreement
would be impossible.

While the discussions are going on in the byre, the youths of the
bridegroom's village charge into the homestead, chanting and
skirmishing as they come. They rush the kraal and the bridegroom hurls his spear at his mother-in-law's *buor*, while the girls
of the bride's village attack the visiting youths in mock combat
and try to catch the bridegroom and seize his wedding stick. If
they succeed he will have to pay them a calf. The *buor* is a mud
windscreen, such as every Nuer woman has in front of her fire-
place outside her hut. It is the symbol of domesticity and of wifely
status and is associated with the spirit of the husband's lineage.
On the occasion of the marriage of a daughter of the hut the windscreen is heightened, or a new one is constructed, for the bridegroom to spear, and some of his close kinsmen may spear it also.
It is easily repaired. The spear belongs to the mother of the bride,
but as it is a war spear one of the men of her homestead grabs
it. The bridegroom has already given, or promised, her a pipe,
tobacco, and a smaller spear, which she may give to a small son
or keep for scraping hides. The bridegroom may also throw a
spear into the threshold of the byre. This goes to his father-in-law.
Other parties of youths from nearby villages are by this time
beginning to arrive, for the wedding was announced by drums on
the previous day. It is difficult for the older people, still talking in
the byre and puffing away at their pipes and drinking beer, to hold
up the dance any longer. They give permission for it to begin, and
it continues for the rest of the afternoon and well into the night
and is resumed on the following morning.

Before the dance begins, or as soon as it has begun, the kin on either side signify their approval of the marriage by calling out the spear-names of the clans or maximal lineages of the bride and bridegroom and invoking the ghosts of their ancestors to look upon the cattle of the bridewealth—a rite which makes the ghosts partners to the union and witnesses of it. The master of ceremonies of the bride—his role is ritual and he has no part in the bride-wealth talks—rises and demands a cow and receives the promise of a calf or sheep. He then walks up and down the byre, brandishing his spear and delivering a long address. He shouts out his ox-name and spear-name, and he calls on the ghosts of the bride's ancestors to witness that she is married openly with fifty cattle (it is conventional to say this number) and not with shame and by stealth. He says that she will bear her husband a male child. He addresses also the bridegroom's kin, his own kin, and anybody else he feels inclined to bring into his speech, and while talking he pours beer and sprinkles a little tobacco on the floor of the byre, on its threshold, and on the hearth in the centre of it, asking God (*Gwandong*) to take his 'cow', the tobacco. Then the master of ceremonies of the bridegroom's family, whose role is also purely ritual, has his say, or he may speak first. He talks in much the same vein and also pours out beer and sprinkles tobacco as an offering as he walks up and down the byre brandishing instead of a spear a wedding stick. The father of the bride may then speak and may be followed by a senior kinsman of the bridegroom. Afterwards people chant poems.

During the dance another rite, but not of the same importance, takes place. The father of the bride removes a tethering cord from one of the pegs in the kraal and throws it into the air between two lines of men drawn up for the purpose, the bride's relatives on one side and the bridegroom's relatives on the other. They try to hook it in the air with their spears and clubs, and whoever catches it may demand a calf or a goat from the opposite side, though he cannot be sure of receiving it.

Towards sunset, or on the following morning, the wedding ox, provided by the bride's father, is sacrificed by the master of ceremonies of her family or a senior kinsman. He rubs ashes on its back and speaks to it, saying: 'We do not kill you for an evil thing, we kill you about a good thing. Fall well.' It is a wedding ox and not a funeral ox. The meat, except for the head, neck, and a few other bits, goes to the bridegroom's kin who, as in the betrothal ceremony, divide the carcass, on the pattern of bridewealth distribution, between the kin on the father's side and those on the mother's side. The distribution of meat at these ceremonies depends on the number of relationships represented by persons or proxy, the number of persons standing in these relationships, and other circumstances. Most of it is taken back by the bridegroom's people to their homes for the older people who have not been able to attend the wedding and those who have remained to look after the herds and milk the cows. The rest is eaten on the spot.

A large part of the night is spent in dancing and flirting and love-making. The bride and the girls of her homestead are cooking while the bridegroom, who is fasting, is seeing that his companions are being properly looked after. On the following morning beer is served, pots being distributed to the bridegroom's kin—his father, his father's full brother, his father's half-brother, his paternal and maternal aunts, and his mother's full and half-brothers—who share the beer with members of their age-sets. After a meal the youths resume dancing and their elders, fortified with beer, probably start once more on the seemingly endless cattle talks, for there are generally an odd claim or two outstanding, the discussion of which was interrupted by the wedding dance, though their settlement was assured before it began.

If the maternal uncle of the bride lives far away he may give a wedding dance on his own account and sacrifice an ox at it. He may even do this when the father and he are members of the same large village. The senior paternal uncle occasionally does the same if he lives far away and is the father's half-brother.

The *ngut* does not conclude the marriage. It is the *mut* and the birth of a child which do this. But the chances are now greatly in favour of a successful conclusion, for had the bride's people not been satisfied with the bridewealth already handed over, or promised, they would not have allowed the dance to proceed. The wedding has also cost them a second ox for which there is no return in the event of the marriage not being consummated. Nevertheless, marriages do occasionally break up between wedding and consummation, though, in my experience, this is rare and is due to the reluctance of the bride rather than to objections or demands on the part of her family and kin.

The *mut*, the third of the three public marriage ceremonies, is the one which, at any rate among the eastern Nuer,* makes the union legally binding. After it the husband, as he can then be called, can claim compensation for adultery, which he could not have done before. Previously the bride's brothers did not feel it obligatory to prevent her from attending evening dances in the neighbourhood, though they well knew from their own experience that she was likely to have relations with her old sweethearts at them. Her future husband's people could not then complain if she attended these dances, whereas after the *mut* they would make an unpleasant scene were they to find her at one, for this ceremony makes man and wife, and the cattle which have been paid are no longer regarded as a pledge but as marriage cattle. They now say of the bride '*Te yang jokde*', 'She has a cow (cattle) on her back.' Moreover, if cattle paid to the bride's family and kin die in their kraals before the *mut*—and they may all die in a year of rinderpest —they have to be replaced by the bridegroom's people, whereas if they die after the *mut* they still count as part of the bridewealth and the husband's people do not have to substitute for them similar beasts. This distinction does not apply to animals killed by the bride's family and kin or which have been disposed of by them and have died outside their kraals, for these count as bridewealth before, as well as after, the consummation. On the other hand, any calves the cattle may bear before this ceremony count as original bridewealth and not as increment. Likewise, if the incomplete union is broken before the *mut*, all the cattle and their increase, including those which have died, must be returned, whereas in the event of divorce after the *mut*, the bride's people do not have to return animals which have died a natural death in their own kraals, and they have a right to retain two cows, the *yang yani* and the *yang miemne*, the cow of the skirts, the mark of married status, and the cow of the hairs, which are shaved off the bride's head at the consummation.

It is *mut*, therefore, which makes the union a contract. Consequently, it occasionally happens, when people are anxious to expedite the marriage, that the consummation takes place before the wedding. I heard it suggested that this should be done in the case of a youth who had been speared and could not take the

* Among the western Nuer it would seem to be the *twoc ghok*, the invocation of the ghosts, which permits a suit of adultery and may therefore be considered the action which makes the union a contract.

iv. Sweethearts

bridegroom's usual part in weddings, and although it was decided to hold the wedding first, with the bridegroom as a spectator, no one suggested that in the circumstances a reversal of the ceremonies would have been improper. Mrs. Smith, of the American Mission, told me of a case of an elderly man who, desiring to marry a girl with the approval of her family but against her own wishes, prevailed on her relatives to rush her through the *mut*, leaving the wedding to be held later.

The day of the consummation has to be fixed in advance because beer has to be brewed for the visitors. In the early morning the bridegroom goes with a company of the youths of his village to fetch the bride, his womenfolk remaining behind to prepare for their visitors. They chant on the way, for this is a happy occasion for the village. Sometimes they find on arrival that the bride's mother has prepared beer for them. They have to ask her permission to take her daughter away and she asks them for presents before she gives it, such things as a spear, armlets, a pipe, and tobacco. The young men promise to give her what she asks for and depart, escorting the bride and her girl companions, who have oiled and decked themselves with ornaments for the ceremony. They go chanting to the bridegroom's village, one of the poems often being a composition of the bride in honour of her future husband, and there is much horseplay between the sexes. When they near the village the young men go ahead and the girls are met by the youths of the village, who bring them into the kraal where they serenade the bridegroom's mother with poems outside her hut. The ceremony is mostly a female affair, the men looking on.

After a while a kinsman of the bridegroom places a tethering-cord across the inner threshold of one of the huts and the bridegroom crawls over it, followed by the bride, the best man, and a special girl friend of the bride. This action is said to make the marriage fruitful. Then, towards evening, takes place the rite of consummation, though there is no invariable order of events in these ceremonies and no fixed time-table. The bride retires to a hut wearing a special goatskin cap and here the bridegroom joins her. His age-mates seek him out and say to him: 'Come now, let the people go to bed, come and loosen the bride's girdle.' He is bashful and gets the business over as quickly and inconspicuously as he can. He enters the hut and gives his bride a cut with a switch and seizes her thigh, she refusing his advances and crouching by the wall of the hut. He strikes her with a tethering-cord, snatches the cap off her head, breaks her girdle, and consummates the marriage. Reluctance is imposed on her by custom and she pretends to resist even when she has known her husband often before in the gardens. It is not expected that a bride will be a virgin. Wedding and consummation ceremonies are held even for a girl who is pregnant or one who has been divorced and is being married a second time if she has not borne children. They say that 'She has returned to maidenhood'. It is only divorced women who have led profligate lives who are not remarried with these ceremonies. Maidenhood is a social, not a physical, state.

His duty done, the bridegroom leaves the hut, sometimes the bride's girl friends rushing at him and beating him with their fists as he emerges. The rest of the evening is given to the favourite pastimes of Nuer youth, *muong* and *lum*, visiting with the girls and making love to them. There will be many youths present: the people of the bridegroom's homestead, his mother's kin, if they live near, youths of the village, and bands of youths from villages for miles around, for the *mut* is a popular ceremony and it is known that many girls will attend it. Then all retire for the night, the bride's companions sleeping in a hut reserved for them.

On the following morning take place three rites which may on no account be omitted, the sacrifice (which may take place the evening before), the lustration, and the shaving of the bride's head. The sacrificial beast should be an ox, but if the bridegroom's father is poor, and at this stage of the marriage he is likely to be hard up, the 'cow of the consummation' may be a goat, or even just beer. The bridegroom's master of ceremonies rubs ashes on its back, calls out his spear-name, and speaks of the beast and the bride, telling the spirits and ghosts of his lineage to witness the union and to bless it with sons so that the lineage may continue. He says to them, 'Now you see your ox; you see this maid; let her be a good wife; let her bear many children, many sons; let her work well in her husband's home, milk the cows, dry the cattle dung; let her be a faithful wife and not a profligate'; and so forth, asking them to make the union a lasting and happy one. He then spears the ox and it is cut up by the wife's people, the visitors, and divided among them in the customary portions, only the head, neck, and a few other pieces of meat going to the people of the bridegroom. The visiting maidens at once cook and eat the ribs, kidneys, and stomach, besides filling themselves with porridge and beer, the bride alone abstaining because she may not eat in the home of her mother-in-law. They take the rest of the carcass back to their homes for their elders. The master of ceremonies may perform another duty associated with his office in anointing the bride with butter. Her father will already have blessed her in this manner before she set out for her husband's home.

Now takes place the rite of lustration, the *lak tetni ka cik*, the washing of the hands with bracelets. The visiting maidens, the young wife's companions, sit in a hut and a pot of warm water is passed to them. One of them washes her hands in the water and then takes a bracelet off her arm, drops it into the pot, and passes the pot to one of the husband's kinsfolk outside, who, squatting in front of it, likewise washes his hands in the water, and then fishes out the bracelet. The pot is returned to the hut and a different maiden and a different kinsman repeat the action of the first pair. All the close kinsfolk of the husband—his father's brothers and sisters, his mother's brothers and sisters, and his own brothers and sisters, and so on—are supposed to receive a bracelet, but, in fact, persons standing in some of these relationships will be absent. Any person who can claim kinship with the husband can demand a bracelet. If a man's dip into the pot reveals a poor bracelet he does not hesitate to upbraid the girl who put it there and he may select a better one from those on her arm.

The concluding rite of the ceremony is the act from which it derives its name, the shaving of the wife's head (*mut nyier*) by a member of her husband's family. This may take place after the departure of her companions, for it is a domestic affair of the husband's family, of which the wife is now a member. The shaving of the head signifies this change in her status. People speak of the rite as 'the removal of the hairs of maidenhood', and they say afterwards of the girl '*Ca ciek*', 'She has become a wife'. She is at the same time stripped of all her ornaments, which are divided among her husband's kin, and she is arrayed in new finery provided by her husband. She belongs to his, and not her father's, people now and it is for them to adorn her.

The *mut* is the consummation of marriage, but not its completion, which is the birth of a child. The young wife is now called *ciek ma kau*, a newly-wed. Her parents give her a hut of her own and a sleeping-hide, a brush, and a couple of gourds for ablutions. When her husband comes to visit her in her father's homestead he sleeps with her in this hut. She continues in all other respects to lead the life she led before marriage, and after her husband's visits she hangs up the hide and domestic utensils and sleeps with her unmarried sisters. On these visits her husband stays at a neighbouring homestead as he cannot eat in the home of his parents-in-law and ought not to be seen there at all. When someone tells the wife that her husband has come, so that she may prepare for him, she feigns annoyance or lack of interest, pretending that she is still unmarried, a shyness she keeps up with third persons, though she is at ease when alone with her husband. When everyone is asleep he visits her and spends the night with her, leaving before any of the bride's people are about. Her parents are supposed to know nothing of his visits, though, of course, they know all about his movements, and it is even said that his mother-in-law may rise especially early and squint through a crack in the door of her hut to see him depart. I was told that should he oversleep and his mother-in-law see his spears outside her daughter's hut, she makes them forfeit, and he would be ashamed to ask for them back. It is not till a child has been born that the husband is accepted by his wife's people as one of themselves. He is then the father of their daughter's child and through the child has a kind of kinship with them. Till this happens the husband continues to lead the life he lived before marriage, a bachelor life with his younger brothers in their father's byre. His wife visits him only on rare occasions and for a formal purpose, as when, at harvest time, she brings him coverings she has made for the grain on the drying-platforms, or when she takes him a bundle of well-cooked porridge made from the first millet of the year—a pretty custom known as *puthene kuan*, honouring with porridge.

All are equally anxious for a child to be born, the husband and wife because they want a son, and the wife's parents and kin because they cannot, without risking complications, dispose of the cattle of the marriage till a first-born completes the union. Those whose daughters they might wish to marry would not be happy about accepting such cattle as bridewealth in case they had suddenly to be returned to the husband. When a child is born the mother remains with her parents till she has weaned it. This is a suitable regulation, because after bridewealth has been paid the husband's father is likely to be short of lactating cows, while the wife's parents will have plenty of milk from their herd. If, for some reason, the wife goes to live with her husband before the child is weaned, it may not be weaned without the consent of her parents, and I have seen a husband pay several cattle to atone for contravention of this rule. A *keagh*, first child, belongs to *cieng mandongni*, the home of his maternal grandparents, and if he is weaned in his father's home he returns to live with them, a boy till he is initiated and a girl till she is betrothed. This is the rule, though there is variation in practice, depending on the ability of the maternal grandparents to support the child and on the relations between them and their son-in-law.

Shortly after the birth of her first-born the wife, now called *paidap*, a nursing mother, brings the baby to her husband's home and lays him in the ashes of the hearth in the centre of his grandfather's byre, a rite known as *nong puka*, the bringing to the ash. Beer has been prepared and is drunk by a few senior kinsmen of the husband who live in his hamlet. It is a domestic, and not a public, ceremony. The wife spends a few days in her husband's home, and returns with the child to the village of her parents. She has as yet no hut of her own in her husband's homestead.

When his first-born has been weaned the husband builds his wife a hut in his father's homestead facing the family kraal. He then goes to ask his parents-in-law for his wife. They do not deny him, even if, as is likely, some of the bridewealth cattle are still owing. They give her a horn spoon and a gourd and she takes these with her to her husband's home. The gift of a spoon is emphasized by Nuer in speaking of marriage, because it is a recognition that the woman is now, in the full sense, a wife, who will eat of the porridge of her own gardens with the milk of her own herd. She now milks her husband's cows instead of her father's and hoes the gardens of his home and not those of her childhood. Before she is given a spoon, even if she hoes a garden at her husband's home she takes the harvest back to her father, or she may live at her husband's home and cultivate in her father's village, if it is not far. It is only when a man's bride has borne him a child and tends his hearth that she becomes, in the Nuer sense, his wife. She then makes a mud windscreen, and the spirit of his lineage comes to dwell there. Later his father tells him to build a byre and gives him a few cows to start a herd.

The marriage has thus reached completion through many stages: betrothal ceremony, wedding ceremony, consummation ceremony, the birth of a child, the bringing of the first-born to his father's byre, and the presentation to the wife' of a spoon as a sign of her domestic separation from her family. She comes to her husband's home not as a wife but as a mother whose breasts have suckled a child of their lineage.

III

Like many other African peoples the Nuer marry by the family and kin of the bridegroom handing over cattle to the family and kin of the bride. The marriage is brought about by this payment and by the performance of the series of ceremonial acts I have just described. These ceremonies and payments of cattle proceed *pari passu* as inter-connected movements towards the completion of the union. It should be remembered that Nuer do not consider the union to be complete till a child has been born of it, even though spouses may continue to cohabit where the union proves to be unfruitful.

I first describe the principles on which bridewealth is paid. These can be simply stated. In actual marriages the payment and distribution of the cattle may be complicated, but if one asks a Nuer how, on marriage, the bridewealth is divided, he gives at once its ideal distribution and it will be found that actual distribution in any particular marriage is made to approximate as far as possible to this ideal. Consequently, once the general principles of transfer are understood, the distribution of cattle on any particular marriage can be readily understood also.

Bridewealth should consist of 40 head of cattle. Among the eastern Nuer 20 are said to go *kwi gwan*, to the father's side, and 20 *kwi man*, to the mother's side, of the bride. Equal division between the bride's paternal kinsmen (including her father) and her maternal kinsmen (including her mother) is thus the first rule of distribution. Of the 20 beasts which go to the father's side, 10 remain with the father (or his sons) and 10 are divided among his family (his parents, brothers, and sisters); and of the 20 beasts which go to the mother's side, 10 remain with the mother (or her sons) and 10 are divided among her family (her parents and brothers and sisters). The second rule, therefore, is that the cattle are distributed in fixed proportions between three families: the bride's own family, her father's family, and her mother's family. The bride's own family receive 20 head of cattle, which are known as the *ghok dieth*, the cattle of parenthood. The families of the bride's father and of her mother each receive 10 head of cattle, known collectively as the *ghok cungni rar*, the cattle of the outside claimants, i.e. those who are outside the bride's own family. It should be noted in the diagram below, in which these distributions are shown, that the bride's mother's sons count as maternal relatives while her father's sons by a different mother count as her paternal relatives.

However, a Nuer does not state such distributions in terms of families but, when he is discussing the mode of distribution, in

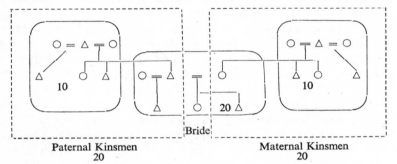

Paternal Kinsmen
20

Bride

Maternal Kinsmen
20

terms of individual relationships and, when he is discussing particular marriages, in reference to persons standing in these relationships. Relationships are defined by reference to the bride. A Nuer counts the ideal distribution as follows:

	Cattle	Total
KWI GWAN (on the paternal side)		
Gwan (father)	A cow and its calf, a cow and its calf, an ox, another ox, a cow, and a calf	8
Gat gwan (father's son)	A cow, and another cow	2
Gwanlen (indit) kwi mane or kwi dwiel (father's elder brother by the same mother)	A cow and its calf, a calf, and an ox	4
Gwanlen kwi gwane or kwi luak (father's brother by a different mother)	A cow and its calf, and an ox	3
Gwanlen (intot) kwi mane or kwi dwiel (father's younger brother by the same mother)	A cow, and an ox	2
Wac (father's sister)	A heifer	1
		20

KWI MAN (on the maternal side)	Cattle	Total
Man (mother)	A cow and its calf and a heifer	3
Deman (brother by the same mother)	An ox, another ox, a cow, another cow, a cow and its calf, and another cow	7
Nar (indit) kwi mane or kwi dwiel (mother's elder brother by the same mother)	A cow and its calf, another cow, and an ox	4
Nar kwi gwane or kwi luak (mother's brother by a different mother)	A cow and its calf, and an ox	3
Nar (intot) kwi mane or kwi dwiel (mother's younger brother by the same mother)	A cow and its calf	2
Manlen (mother's sister)	A heifer	1
		20

I do not guarantee that if one were to ask any Nuer from the eastern part of their territory how bridewealth is distributed in his country he would receive a list identical with the one I have given, for there might be shifts here and there of a cow or an ox, but the balance and proportions would be as I have recorded them. Among the western Nuer, when a man speaks of 'the cattle on the paternal side' and 'the cattle on the maternal side' his description is more in accord with realities because he includes among 'the cattle on the paternal side' those beasts which go to the bride's mother and uterine brother, since the father gets them if he is alive. The western Nuer way of counting bridewealth is therefore less symmetrical than the eastern way of counting it. This difference is superficial, because in all parts of Nuerland the same relationships are a title to approximately the same number of cattle.

The persons who have, in virtue of one of these emphasized relationships, a right (cuong) to cattle are called the ji cungni, the people with a right. They say: 'Manlen a cuong', 'The maternal aunt has a right'; 'Wac a cuong', 'The paternal aunt has a right', and so on. The cattle which the various relatives of the bride will receive in a perfect distribution, each according to his right, are indicated below:

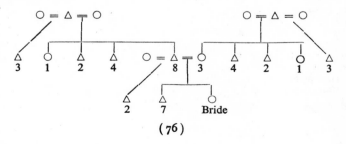

It must be added that the four grandparents of the bride are entitled each to a cow, called *wangnen*, in certain circumstances, but they are not mentioned in the distribution given above because it is assumed that by the time their granddaughter is old enough to be married they will be dead. It is a rule that in the event of any claimant being dead his, or her, sons inherit the right to cattle. Thus the cattle of a *gwanlen* (father's brother) go to the *gaatgwanlen* (father's brother's sons), the cattle of a *wac* (father's sister) go to the *gaatwac* (father's sister's sons), and so forth. But whereas cattle must be paid, whatever may be the circumstances, to the names of these kinsmen, a grandparent only receives a cow if he, or she, saw the bride before he, or she, died. It is possible, therefore, for there to be four *wangnen* claims, but there are generally only one or two at most. The *wangnen* of the father's father goes to one of his sons by a different mother to the father's mother. The *wangnen* of the father's mother goes to one of her sons other than the father. These are the *wangnen kwi gwane*, the cows of the grandparents on the paternal side. There may also be two *wangnen kwi mane*, cows of the grandparents on the maternal side, that of the mother's father going to one of his sons by a different mother to the bride's mother's mother, and that of the mother's mother going to one of her sons. Thus in the diagram below, A's cow goes to M, B's cow goes to N, C's cow goes to O, and D's cow goes to P. As will be explained later, these cattle of the grandparents are not paid in addition to the forty already listed.

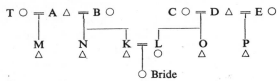

Some features of this mode of distribution are worth attention. The cattle are divided among both paternal and maternal relatives of the bride and this bilateral distribution may be wrongly interpreted. It is by no means simply a recognition of the bride's kinship to certain of her kinsfolk, but is also an acknowledgement of obligation between siblings and towards affines. The payment to the bride's paternal uncles is not only an expression of the relationship between a father's brother and his brother's daughter, but also of that between brother and brother. A man marries from the family herd in which his brothers have equal rights with himself, and his wife is, as the brothers say, 'our wife', because she was married with 'our cattle'. She acts in domestic duties as a wife to her husband's unmarried brothers as well as to her husband, although she cohabits with him alone, and her children are all 'our children' since they are 'children of our cattle'. All the brothers therefore have rights in the daughters of each. Brothers stubbornly insist on these rights, and it often happens that a girl's paternal uncle proves to be the most serious obstacle to bringing about her marriage, for he will not hesitate to veto it if he thinks he is not getting his fair share of the cattle. Every Nuer knows exactly where he stands in such matters, for even children know how bridewealth ought to be distributed and can at once tell roughly what cattle each kinsman will receive on the marriage of the daughter of one of them.

Likewise the transfers made to the bride's maternal uncles are not only an expression of the relationship between a mother's brother and his sister's daughter, but also of that between a man and his wife's brother. Nuer stress that at marriage only part of what is due to the bride's family is handed over to them and say that the rest will be paid when their daughter has borne female children and these children are married. The extra-family kinsmen, the paternal and maternal uncles and aunts of the bride, receive their share of her bridewealth once and for all at her marriage, often at the expense of the intra-family kinsmen, her parents and brothers and sisters, who will, in compensation, receive in addition to what is paid to them at her marriage some ten head of cattle on the marriage of each of her daughters. It must not be forgotten that the maternal uncles and aunts of the bride are the brothers-in-law and the sisters-in-law of her father, and that the part of her bridewealth paid to them is to some extent considered as a deferred payment incurred at her mother's marriage. Hence Nuer, when counting the cattle to be paid on marriage, conclude by saying: 'And when the bride's daughters are married more cattle will be paid to their mother's brothers.' It should be noted also that the sibling relationship is acknowledged in the distribution of bridewealth on the maternal as on the paternal side. All the brothers have rights in their sister and in that part of the bridewealth of her daughters which is due to their family. Here again, even small boys know their rights as maternal uncles, or as future maternal uncles, and youths regard them as policies which will fall due in the future and enable them to marry wives themselves.

We must distinguish, in discussing the transmission of bride-wealth among the Nuer, between the transfer of cattle by the bridegroom's people and its distribution among the kinsfolk of the bride. The bridegroom's people are only interested in this distri-bution in so far as it affects the total of cattle they will have to pay. They come to the lengthy negotiations which precede the wedding dance prepared to pay a certain number of beasts, and so long as their estimate is not exceeded it is a matter of little interest to them what arrangements about their distribution the kinsmen of the bride make among themselves. The bride's father must make his own terms about the distribution with his brothers and sisters, and the bride's senior maternal uncle with his brothers and sisters. The necessity for them to come to some agreement among them-selves will be evident later.

Another important feature of bridewealth distribution is the distinction made between sons of the mother (*gaatman*) and sons of the father (*gaatgwan*). This distinction is made not only between the full and half-brothers of the bride but also between the full and half-brothers of her father and mother. In the genera-tion of her uncles the differentiation between full and half-brothers is indicated by stating whether they are uncles *kwi mane*, on the mother's side, or *kwi gwane*, on the father's side; the terms *kwi dwiel* on the side of the hut, and *kwi luak*, on the side of the byre, being commonly employed as alternative indications. The statement of the ideal distribution thus assumes polygamous families.

When the father of the bride is alive the distinction between her full and half-brothers is only formally represented in the division of her bridewealth because the cattle given to any of her brothers join their father's herd and he uses them as is customary, which means that they are held as family stock from which each son marries in order of seniority, being given by his father for this purpose what cattle are available, without regard to the title by which they entered the herd. Thus one son may marry with cattle which were allotted to another son in the distribution of their sister's bridewealth; so the fact that on the marriage of one of the sisters several cattle are allotted to the uterine brother does not mean that he can dispose of them as he pleases, and he would not, were his father alive, be able to reserve them for his own marriage exclusively. If the bride's half-brother is older than he the half-brother will use some of these cows to marry and no objection can be raised to his doing so. To object would, in Nuer eyes, be a grave breach of custom amounting to the breaking up of the family and home and the severing of vital bonds of kinship. Even after the father is dead the herd ought to remain common stock, and all cattle accruing to him and his sons on the marriages of his daughters ought to join it for the benefit of all his sons alike, so that they may marry from it in order of seniority. If there is only one widow this is likely to happen, but when there are several widows the family often breaks up, the widows going with their children to live in different places, and the herd may in course of time become scattered. Eventually the family, especially the composite or polygamous family, ceases to have corporate interests in a common herd and splits into a number of property units, each brother having a family and herd of his own. The brothers then live in separate homesteads and sometimes in separate villages, and the cattle they receive as paternal and maternal uncles therefore join different herds. Often some of the brothers are by this time dead and the cattle then go to their sons, whose ties with their paternal uncles are weaker than those uniting brothers.

In reckoning the cattle which have to be transferred Nuer distinguish between those beasts which receive a precise linguistic indication and the remainder. Those terminologically differentiated are regarded as the minimum payment on which negotiations can start. Whatever else the bride's family and kin get, they must get certain animals or the marriage cannot take place. Hence these basic claims take precedence and their titles are always the first to be acknowledged. The conventional order is as follows:

1. *wangnen gwane*, the cows of the paternal grandparents.
   wangnen mane, the cows of the maternal grandparents.

2. *yang gwane kene doude, ke thakde,* the cow of the father with its calf, and his ox.
   yang mane kene doude, the cow of the mother with its calf.

3. *yang gwanlene kene doude, ke thakde,* the cow of the paternal uncle with its calf, and his ox.

   yang nara kene doude, kene thakde, ke puangde, the cow

of the maternal uncle with its calf, and his ox, and his
puang (ox).

4. *dou (nac) waca*, the calf (heifer) of the paternal aunt.
    dou (nac) manlene, the cow (heifer) of the maternal aunt.

5. *yang kwoth gwande*, the cow of the father's spirit.
    yang kwoth mande, the cow of the mother's spirit.

6. *thak deman*, the ox of the uterine brother.
    thak gat gwan, the ox of the paternal half-brother.

It will be observed that these titles to cattle are in pairs of
collateral relationships. If a person standing in any one of the
relationships is dead, his claim takes precedence over claims of
the living, and for this reason they generally begin the tally with
the *wangnen* cows of the grandparents. 'First the claims of the
ghosts must be settled, then we can settle the claims of us who
remain alive.' In actual payments of bridewealth the fact that the
kin of the bride are able to claim one or more cows of this title
does not mean that they receive more cattle on this account than
they would otherwise have done. Circumstances, to be discussed
later, fix the total payment within approximate limits known to
both parties to the contract, so that all that happens is that a cow
which would in any case go to one of the bride's uncles as part of
his portion of the bridewealth is handed over to the name of a
dead grandparent.

A few words may be said about the *yang kwoth*, cow of the
spirit, which figures in most bridewealth transactions. This animal
is paid in honour of the spirit of the father or of the mother of the
bride. The spirits are of various kinds. If one of them is a totem
and is associated with a special colour, the bride's parents will
endeavour to obtain from the bridegroom's kin a cow of that
colour, e.g. a tawny cow for the lion-spirit and a brindled cow for
the crocodile-spirit. A cow so dedicated to a spirit must remain in
the kraal of the parents, and now and again they rub ashes along
its back and pour milk over its tethering-peg and invoke the spirit.
The spirits of the family are thus made cognizant of the marriage
and are a party to the pact, just as the ghosts are informed of what
is taking place and are invoked as witnesses at the wedding ceremony. Spirits and ghosts are *jicungni*, claimants entitled to a share
in the bridewealth, and were they to be denied their right the
marriage would not be fruitful. When each parent has a different

spirit both must be honoured by having a cow of the bride-cattle dedicated to it, though one spirit may receive a cow on the marriage of one daughter and the other on the marriage of her sister. Here again, this does not necessarily mean that the family of the bride get an extra cow, for generally one of the cows they would in any case have received is dedicated to a spirit and paid in its name. Sometimes, however, the bride's people do not put forward the claim till the end of the marriage negotiations, when the bridegroom's people think that a settlement has been reached and have already offered as many cattle as they are prepared to give. It is more difficult for them to refuse an extra cow to a spirit than to a man. If they are wise they will get to know all about the spirits of the bride's family—there may be more than two—and anticipate the claim by keeping a cow in reserve to meet it. Generally these essential claims are settled at the first bridewealth discussions held in the byre of the bride's father.

The maternal side of the family have a prior claim to consideration in that, as already explained, their portion is regarded to some extent as a deferred payment standing over from the marriage of the bride's mother. If there are not enough cattle to satisfy everyone at the time of the marriage the paternal relatives are usually prepared to allow the bridegroom to remain for some years in their debt, but the maternal relatives are less willing to forgo immediate satisfaction. The maternal kinsmen cannot make exorbitant demands because they have only a right to a conventional proportion of the bridewealth and the approximate number of cattle to be paid to them is therefore determined by the total number to be paid all round.

In marriages today the actual payments and distributions of cattle to definite persons, as distinct from the ideal allotment of fixed portions of the bridewealth to relationships, vary according to circumstances, the chief of which, apart from the relative desire of both parties to bring about the union, are the wealth in stock of the Nuer as a whole, the resources of the bridegroom's family and kin, the number of claimants and the shares allotted to them in other marriages, and the configuration of the bride's family.

There is good reason to suppose that till thirty to forty years ago cattle were so plentiful in Nuerland that bridewealth was paid at the ideal rate of 40 head. In recent years the herds have diminished through rinderpest, and raids on Dinka stock, the traditional means of recuperation, are prevented by the presence of the Anglo-Egyptian government. Diminution has been fairly uniform throughout the whole of Nuerland, and it would today in all parts be impossible for a man to raise as many as 40 head of cattle for marriage. The usual payment is from 20 to 30. It has been mentioned that there are a number of relationships with basic rights and the persons standing in these relationships, or representing those standing in them, must be guaranteed their portions to the number of cattle enumerated in the list presented above. Consequently, even if there are no *wangnen* and spirit claims, the bridewealth cannot fall to less than 16 beasts. On the other hand, it cannot rise to more than the bridegroom and his people possess or are prepared to give, what they are prepared to give being mainly decided by what they possess. The bridewealth will therefore be somewhere between these two points. Now, the bride's family know fairly accurately what cattle are available and state their demands in the light of their knowledge, and the bridegroom's family know who are likely to put forward claims and, also, how many cattle they can muster, and they make their offer accordingly.

It is evident from the lengthy discussions that continue for hours at a time, and sometimes for days on end, that there is no absolutely fixed payment. What happens is that the basic claims are first settled in a preliminary manner, for there can be little argument about these, and further demands are then debated. The main concern of the bridegroom's party is to conduct the negotiations in such a way that they will not have promised up to the estimate they have allowed for before an adequate number of cattle have been allotted to all the persons who are beyond question entitled to them. They usually aim at settling all the outside claims before tackling the full family claims, in the settlement of which they may expect some forbearance. The family are as anxious as the bridegroom's people to settle the outside claims, for they are claims on the bride's father as much as on the bridegroom, and until they are met he cannot reap any benefit himself from the marriage. To facilitate their settlement the family are generally prepared to forgo some of their own rights and the expectation of full immediate payment.

The discussions are in terms of particular cattle. The bridegroom's people offer certain animals and these animals are known to the bride's people. The spokesman for the bridegroom says, for example, that they have a brindled cow and its calf in such-and-such a kraal, and the spokesman for the family replies that these will be the cow of the mother and its calf. The bridegroom's maternal uncle says that he will give a white cow with a black head and rump and its calf, and a white-faced ox, and the people of the byre decide that the cow and its calf will be the cow of the father and its calf, and the ox will be the ox of the uterine brother. To follow these negotiations it must be remembered that they have been preceded by lengthy private discussions by each party among themselves. The bridegroom's party have agreed among themselves which particular animals each is willing to contribute, what they intend to offer the bride's people, what claims are likely to be put forward, and how they can be met. The bride's party have discussed what animals the other side possess, what they are likely to offer, and what they themselves want. The haggling at the final meetings between the two parties is on the surface and concerns only marginal beasts which the bride's party hope to obtain above what the bridegroom's party wish to give. It is not really greed on one side or parsimony on the other, but part of the traditional procedure of marriage. Both sides are expected to behave in this way in marriage negotiations.

As long as the girl's family receive a good number of the cattle before she has passed through the final ceremonies and can expect that the remainder will eventually be paid they will not press for settlement. Nuer can be very generous in this matter, and if a son-in-law is respectful and industrious they will not break the union because he takes a long time to pay the final cows, for marriage is not simply handing over a girl in exchange for cattle but is the creation of a series of new social relationships which, once formed, are not easily or lightly severed, especially when the union is completed by the birth of a child.

Sometimes the final cows are never paid. If the husband has cattle and his wife's brothers want to marry, they may raid his herd and take the beasts owing to them. But debts of this kind are subject to a rule of limitations. If the cattle have not all been paid before the eldest son of the marriage is initiated into manhood the debt lapses. Therefore a brother tries to obtain the remainder of his sister's bridewealth before this happens. An illustrative case occurred in western Nuerland in 1936. An initiated lad, who had been working for me, brought back three cows to add to the family herd in his father's kraal and his maternal uncle seized one of them on the grounds that his mother's bridewealth had not been fully paid. The elders of the village counselled its return, saying that the calves would die, and their advice was taken. The opinion expressed on this occasion was that when a son is initiated he becomes part-owner of the family herd and that a maternal uncle cannot take cattle from the herd of his sister's son in payment for his sister's marriage. Also, if cattle are owing, claimants cannot take them from the bridewealth of a daughter of the union, that is to say, from cattle allotted to the bride's family. They get their due portions from the daughter's marriage, but 'the cattle of a mother and the cattle of her daughter may not meet'. It is thought that the daughter would be barren were this to happen.

Distribution, as distinct from the total transfer, is also affected by the number of persons who demand cattle. There may be several persons standing to the bride in any given relationship. If, for example, there is only one paternal aunt, she gets her cow on the marriage of each of her brothers' daughters. If, on the other hand, there are several paternal aunts, they take it in turn to receive the cows due to that relationship. Difficulties are sometimes settled between two claimants of like relationship to the bride by one of them taking a cow and the other its first calf. Sometimes they take it in turn to receive their due, and, at the same time, admit the rights of the others to a calf each. In this way each claimant may ultimately receive part of the bridewealth on each occasion of its distribution. On the other hand, there may be no person in the relationship entitled to cattle. In this case, as already explained, a lineal heir is entitled to the beasts; but a collateral kinsman may not inherit. If there is neither a claimant nor a lineal heir other relatives on that side of the family receive larger shares than they would have expected had there been either. To reach an understanding of any actual distribution it is often necessary to relate it to distributions at other marriages, for, especially today when cattle are scarce, consideration will always be given, in seeking a fair agreement, to rights claimed or forgone in previous, and to expectations in future, marriages of daughters of the family and kin.

Paternal kinsmen genealogically farther removed from the bride than those indicated by specific kinship terms (relationships with a fixed title to bridewealth) may claim some small gift, such as a sheep, goat, or spear, in their own right from the bridegroom's people. Though these casual claims count as part of the bride-wealth in that their return can be asked for in the event of divorce, their settlement is regarded more as a courtesy than as an obliga-tion. A borderline case between bride-cattle proper and such small gifts to distant kinsmen is that of the calf, called *karthar* among the western Nuer, which may be claimed by a collateral kinsman who is a patrilineal descendant of the bride's father's father's father. This payment is sometimes made, as a sign that the patri-lineal limit of bridewealth claims has been reached and that no demands will be accepted from collateral kinsmen tracing their common descent with the bride from an ancestor yet farther removed.

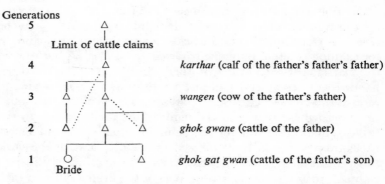

Generations

5 — Limit of cattle claims

4 — *karthar* (calf of the father's father's father)

3 — *wangen* (cow of the father's father)

2 — *ghok gwane* (cattle of the father)

1 — Bride — *ghok gat gwan* (cattle of the father's son)

However, any cognatic kinsman up to six or seven generations removed from a common ancestor with the bride may attest his kinship by asking a small gift, and it will not be refused. This privilege, which is not widely exercised, includes also natural and affinal kin. I have seen a bride's maternal uncle's natural (not legal) son and a bride's paternal uncle's wife's brother demand, and given, spears at marriages. The master of ceremonies of the bride's family is always given a calf, sheep, or goat, known as 'the cow of the spear' (with which he made the invocation).

As said above, actual distribution of bridewealth among persons depends also on the configuration of the bride's family. At this point it need only be said that distribution on the marriage of a daughter born of a simple legal union is the pattern for distribu-tion at marriages of daughters born of other kinds of union. We need only note further that when the genitor of the bride is a different person from her pater, as is often the case among the Nuer, he has a right to a cow, 'the cow of the begetting', and that this takes precedence over all other claims. If he has also brought up the bride his right is more extensive.

I conclude this section on bridewealth with three illustrations of actual payments and distributions at the present time. The first is from the Lou tribe of eastern Nuerland, the second from the Dok tribe of western Nuerland, and the third from the Leek tribe of western Nuerland.

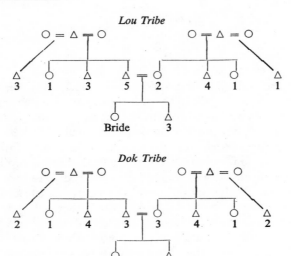

It will be observed from these two examples that in spite of smaller payments today the balance of distribution between paternal and maternal relatives is preserved. It will be noted also that smaller bridewealth does not mean that the rights of the family take precedence over those of the extra-family kinsmen. On the contrary, the family bear the greater proportional loss. In the Lou marriage the family received only 10 out of 23 beasts and in the Dok marriage only 8 out of 22 (the calf received by the master of ceremonies in each case not being included in the reckoning). The uncles and aunts must always be satisfied and their claims settled first, so that if there is to be a loss or debt the family must bear it. This conclusion was borne out by records of payments in other marriages.

I now examine in greater detail a payment of 23 beasts in a marriage in the Leek tribe to show the kind of considerations which affect distribution of bridewealth in particular marriages. At the time of my inquiries the marriage had been consummated but a child had not been born.

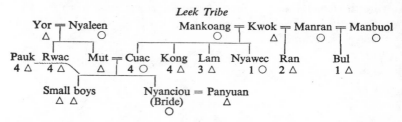

Leek Tribe

Pauk, the biological father of the bride, received three beasts in addition to 'the cow of the begetting'. There were two reasons for this generosity: he had brought the bride up from birth, and he was living with her mother and kept his cattle with hers. He was, in fact, acting as husband and father in the bride's family, and since he had no family of his own the bride's small brothers (not named in the chart) were regarded as his heirs. He had begotten them also. So the family received in fact eight beasts and not just the four shown in the chart, which, the father being dead, were allocated to the names of father and mother jointly. It was agreed also that the bride's eldest brother should receive a cow (not listed in the chart) before the eldest son of Nyanciou's marriage to Panyuan is initiated. Rwac, the bride's paternal uncle, received in addition to the three animals held to be the right of the paternal uncle in the discussions preceding the marriage a fourth beast, the cow of the paternal aunt, since there was no one standing in this relationship to the bride. This was not an inherited right but a device for ensuring that the father's side to the marriage received their fair quota of cattle. Such adjustments are common in division of bridewealth. In other respects distribution on this occasion was normal and requires no further comment.

It may be noted, however, that though the allocation of cattle was as I have just stated it the full brothers of the bride's mother had not yet received their shares of the bridewealth. The reason for this was that the bride was not living with her paternal kinsmen, who took little interest in her, but she and her mother were living in the village of her maternal kinsmen, from which she was married. The paternal kinsmen therefore in this instance received the cattle immediately available for distribution. Had the bride been living with her paternal kin the maternal uncles would not have been so accommodating. It may further be noted that whereas the maternal half-uncles had received their share of the cattle, the senior maternal full uncle had received up to the time when my inquiries were made none of the animals promised to him and the junior maternal full uncle was still owed a heifer. The maternal half-uncles had to be given their shares first because if any debt is incurred it must be borne by those primarily responsible for the marriage agreement and chiefly in control of its arrangements, in this case the bride's full maternal uncles in whose village she was living. The single example I have given will, I hope, be sufficient to show how various circumstances may influence any actual distribution of bridewealth.

IV

In the account I have given of bridewealth it was brought out that there are two connected, but separate, movements in its transfer: the payment by the bridegroom's kin to the bride's kin, and the further division of the cattle among the bride's relations. I feel that it would be profitable here to make some further comments on the first movement in order to elucidate the general functions of bridewealth in Nuer society.

It is no longer necessary to show that the African payment of bridewealth is not a purchase. But to say that it is not price or purchase is not to say that the objects handed over have no significance outside the particular purpose they serve in bringing about a union. Cattle for Nuer are one of the main sources of food and they supply many other domestic requirements, they have a prestige value, and they have religious importance. The payment or receipt of bridewealth changes a man's fortune in a very material way. The bridegroom's family are impoverished, sometimes to the point of privation, though their kinsmen and affines will help them if they reach this point; while in the bride's home the milk-gourds and butter-gourds are full. A man who receives only one cow of the bridewealth has in it the promise of a herd.

It is for this reason that Nuer found it difficult to understand what I meant when I told them that among my people we marry without paying bridewealth: 'It does not matter. After all, every country has its own customs. But is it right that the father and mother of your wife should go empty-handed when you marry, or is it better that they should be full, that the father should be full and the mother full?' Of the neighbouring Anuak people, who marry with beads and spears, they say: 'Of what use are these things? Can people live on them?' In making their demands on the bridegroom's people the bride's people try to obtain above all lactating cows and their calves or heifers in-calf so that they may enjoy immediate benefit from the transaction.

Nevertheless, Nuer men show greater interest in the bride-wealth character of cattle than in their nutritive qualities. It is not that having great nutritive value they acquire through it a general social value, become a standard of worth, and are therefore employed in ritual, for indemnification of injury, and as a means of acquiring a mate. It is rather that their use as bridewealth gives them their supreme value in Nuer eyes. Cattle stand for a wife and are therefore the most important thing in a Nuer's life, because a wife means to him his own home and that he becomes a link in the lineage by fathering a son. Nuer do not grudge the loss of a herd to obtain a wife. They lose cattle, but the wife will bear them daughters at whose marriages the cattle will return, and sons who will herd them.

It is therefore a common-sense inference that payment of bride-wealth has a stabilizing action in marriage. If the wife leaves her husband the cattle will have to be returned, and as it would be always unpleasant, and often difficult, to return them it might be supposed that the wife's family will use their influence to make her remain with her husband. There is some truth in this supposition, for Nuer know only too well the confusion, and consequent resentment, that may result from the dissolution of a marriage: 'But with us Nuer, if a wife leaves her husband what will his kinsmen do? For they have given some of the cattle to her paternal uncles, some to her maternal uncles, some to her paternal aunt, and some to her maternal aunt. A wife should be obedient to her husband, for she has been married with cattle.' It must be remembered that not only have the cattle to be returned but their calves also—I have known a divorce in which one of the bridewealth cows had to be returned with no less than eight calves—and as these may have been widely dispersed much altercation may ensue. Indeed, one of the earliest British officers in Nuerland wrote that 'the system of marriage among the Nuers is the cause of nearly all their quarrels and troubles'.* Everyone concerned with the marriage stands to lose by its dissolution and they will try to prevent divorce.

Nevertheless, it can only be accepted that payment of bridewealth stabilizes marriage to a very limited degree. That this is so can best be understood by considering the question in relation to what happens at divorce. The marriage tie is severed by the return of the bridewealth because either the wife has died childless or her husband's people give up their rights in her. In either case, if there are no children, all the cattle have to be returned, except 'the cow (ox) of the hairs and the cow of the skirts',† unless they have died a natural death in the homesteads of the recipients. If the wife dies after bearing a single living child the usual procedure is for the extra-family kinsmen to return their portions of the bridewealth and for the family of the wife to retain their portions, the child remaining with his father. If the wife leaves her husband after the birth of their first-born his kin may decide to claim the return of their bridewealth except for six head of cattle, which the husband leaves with his wife's people to retain his rights in the child (*ruok*). These six beasts, including the two of 'the hairs and the skirts', are kept by the family of the wife. The extra-family kinsmen lose their portions of the bridewealth. The wife by this procedure is divorced and can remarry. On the other hand, they may leave all their cattle with the wife's family and kin and maintain thereby their rights in any children she may 'bear in the bush', that is, by lovers. She is then not divorced, but is only separated, from her husband, and she cannot remarry.

I was told that if a wife dies after having borne two children no cattle are returned, it being held that 'cattle which have children

---

* Bimbashi H. Gordon, *Sudan Intelligence Reports*, June 1903, No. 107.

† According to my own information these two animals are always retained by the bride's parents should the marriage be broken up after the consummation ceremony and are regarded in some part as payment for loss of the bride's maidenhood at the consummation and in some part as compensation for the expenses of the nuptial ceremonies. Mr. H. C. Jackson (*Sudan Notes and Records*, vol. vi, 1923, p. 155) says that they are left with the parents only if the husband is responsible for the dissolution of the marriage. Mr. P. P. Howell tells me that he is of the same opinion as Mr. Jackson.

on their backs cannot be returned'. Nuer said that should a wife leave her husband after having borne two children the cattle would remain with her kinsmen and any children she might bear by other men would be claimed by her husband's people. She is still married to him though she lives as concubine to another man. They said that the husband's people would generally be content with this arrangement but, whether content or not, it would be useless for them to ask for return of their cattle and the progeny of these cattle. The wife's people would say to them: 'You have your children. You keep them and we will keep the cattle. Let your wife bear you children in the bush.'

The rules stated above are principles which are flexibly applied according to the circumstances. In cases of divorce much depends on the personal relations between the husband's people and the wife's people. If they are bad and his wife has left him at their instigation, the husband may claim back everything to which he has a right: cattle, sheep, goats, spears, tobacco, millet, and ornaments, including his wife's bead-decorated skirt. But if they are good and she has left her husband against her parents' wishes, he will not ask for the return of the smaller gifts and the *puoth manthude*, the little gifts with which he honoured his mother-in-law; and if she dies childless he may also leave some of the cattle to which he has a right with her parents in the hope that they will later give him her sister in her place, or just from sympathy. If he leaves any of the cattle, preference will be given to the portions of the spirits and the ghosts.

Another contingency which is taken into consideration is whether the wife is being sent away by her husband for barrenness or bad habits, which is rare, or whether she is leaving him without his consent and, in this case, whether she has adequate grounds for refusing to live with him, such as neglect or cruelty. Whatever the circumstances are, the husband has a right either to his cattle or to the children his wife may bear to other men, but it sometimes happens that whereas he wants his cattle back to marry again, since he cannot have a home without a wife, the wife's people tell him that he is responsible for the separation and must be satisfied with the children. They would not refuse him his children. If they tell him this—and they would not do so unless she had already borne him a child and had lived in his home—he has to accept their decision. There are no courts he can appeal to

v. Duelling at a dance

and his kinsmen would be unwilling to support him in resort to force. There is nothing he can do. If his wife has gone back to her parents and they do not want to return his cattle they tell him to come and fetch her. But if she is miserable with him she will only run away again, and this time to some distant part of the country. If he complains to her parents they say that it is no affair of theirs. Let him go and get his wife. In the end he will give her up and claim any children she may bear to lovers. There is always a chance that she will come back to him when he takes charge of her sons. I have never known a case in which a wife's parents have refused to return her husband's cattle after they have married her to another man, and when I asked what would happen were they to try to do so, I was told that the husband's kin would undoubtedly use violence to get back their cattle and, in addition, curse the wife so that either she would become barren or her children die. On the other hand, it sometimes happens that the wife's people promise to return the cattle as soon as they are able to do so but fail to return them all, through procrastination on one pretext or another or prevarication, for they may hide some of their cows in the herds of kinsmen in distant districts. If the husband and his wife's father are members of the same local community, difficulties of this kind are not likely to arise and, if they do, they can be settled by discussion and compromise. If the two men belong to different sections of the same tribe, and even more if they belong to different tribes, the dispute, as is the case in all issues of indemnity, is not so easily settled.

We may now consider in the light of these facts to what extent bridewealth may be said to stabilize marriage. Most broken marriages occur during or shortly after the nuptial ceremonies. One cannot properly speak of divorce at this stage because in Nuer eyes marriage is incomplete till a child has been born. That till the birth of a child the wife is considered to belong to her own kin and not to her husband's kin is shown not only in her continuing to live with her parents but in other ways, most noticeably by the fact that the husband is held responsible for her death should she die in her first childbirth. He then has to pay compensation for homicide (*thung yika*). During this period, when the union is looked upon as still only partly formed, the family and kinsmen of the wife do not, if they are wise, disperse the cattle. At this stage, therefore, there is no great difficulty about returning the cattle, which are, indeed, kept ready at hand to be returned should the need arise. Also, it must be remembered that the husband is unlikely to have paid all the bridewealth before a child is born.

I cannot give figures, but on the basis of my observations and of my discussions with Nuer on the subject I would say that when marriage has been brought about through the normal negotiations, payments, and ceremonies, divorce after the wife has brought her first child to her husband's home and has lived with him for a year or two is very unusual. Should it take place the wife's family, who alone can bring much pressure to bear on her, do not, with regard to the reduced payments of bridewealth of the present day, stand to lose much, for they will retain six head of cattle. It is the extra-family kinsmen, who have less influence over the wife, who lose all their cattle.

I have never known, or heard of, a case of divorce, or even of separation, after the birth of a second child. My own observations are very limited, but they are supported by the opinion of Nuer that when man and wife have lived together for several years and have children the wife is most unlikely to leave her husband's home while he is alive. Were she to do so the cattle would not, in any case, as I have explained, be returned. After the birth of his second child a husband ceases to keep track of the progeny of his cattle.

It should be noted that it may happen today that all the cattle in the kraal of the wife's father die of rinderpest shortly after the consummation of the marriage. As we have earlier noted, it is then not incumbent on the husband to replace them, or on his father-in-law to return others in their stead if the wife dies or leaves her husband. The wife's people need only return beasts in the place of those which have died after they have transferred them to third parties or which they have butchered. The father-in-law could not in these circumstances break off the marriage and marry his daughter to another man, for the cattle, though dead, are still 'on the wife's back'. When I asked what would happen were he to try to do so, I was told that the husband's kin would claim back their cattle and if necessary use force to obtain them. Should a wife leave her husband in these circumstances the problem of bridewealth would probably be solved by the common Nuer expedient of letting her live as a concubine.

I think it is evident, in view of the facts stated above, that the fear of having to repay bridewealth cannot be said to be a very powerful sanction of the marriage union. Nor is there any evidence of which I am aware that would suggest that the greater the number of cattle handed over the more stable the marriage is likely to prove. Indeed, I am prepared to say definitely that the stability of Nuer marriage rests on quite other foundations than payments of bridewealth: affection between the spouses, the good reputation of the husband, mutual goodwill between the families of husband and wife, especially personal friendship between the fathers or between the husband and his wife's brother, and moral and legal norms.

It is generally safe to assume that when a woman lives with her husband it is because she chooses to do so and is happy in her marriage. By the time a girl is fully married to a man she knows him well. Usually he has courted her before asking for her hand, and she must give her consent before his request is granted. She has plenty of time between the betrothal ceremony and the ceremony of consummation in which to withdraw from the marriage should she be reluctant to complete it, and yet more time between the consummation and the birth of a child. I do not say that pressure may not be put on her by her family to accept her husband, but Nuer girls are not easily coerced. Nuer have good grounds for their assumption that a newly-wed who has borne her husband a child and brought it to his hearth is satisfied with her mate. By the time a second child is born experience has shown that the pair are agreeable to one another also as domestic partners. As Nuer observe a weaning taboo, this means at least three years after the birth of the first child.

Mutual goodwill between the families is also a necessary condition of a successful marriage. Marriage is not only a conjugal relationship but also a set of affinal relations, and it can be stable only if the kin on both sides behave towards the other side in the manner expected of them. This they endeavour to do. A man tries not only to live up to the pattern of what Nuer regard as a good husband but also to be a polite and helpful son-in-law and his wife's family try to act correctly towards him. The relatives on both sides also try to behave towards those on the other side as persons standing in these relationships should do. It is the evocative and inhibitory action of these moral values, sanctioned by approbation and censure, which give stability to marriage and security to the family that derives from it. Divorce is due to failure of one or other of the parties to live up to the code of conduct expected of him or her, and Nuer regard it as a misfortune in which there is also an element of the shameful.

Conjugal and affinal relations are personal relationships which require adult adjustment that is not easy. A Nuer regulates his behaviour to the persons around him through kinship values of one kind or another. Owing to the extensive area of kinship covered by Nuer marriage prohibitions, a man cannot marry into a family or lineage with whom he has already close kinship ties. He must therefore marry the daughter of people who are under no obligation to provide him with a wife or, indeed, to assist him in any way. This means forging new social links which by their nature cannot at their inception be of a kinship order. Nuer bridewealth payments are thus complementary to their marriage prohibitions.

Eventually affinal ties are, by slow degrees, transformed, as Nuer themselves say, into kinship ties. The birth of a child gives the wife kinship with her husband's people and the husband kinship with his wife's people. They say that *ruagh*, in-law relationship, becomes *mar*, kinship. Bridewealth payments may therefore be viewed as a technique for creating new social relations between persons between whom there are no well-defined patterns of behaviour and for maintaining them. They are one of the many ways in which gifts and payments are used for this purpose, and have this function, in primitive societies. Bridewealth may thus be thought of as providing a kind of social scaffolding, a temporary structure of behaviour patterns, which enables the union to be built up. It ceases to be of any great significance once the new family is firmly established after the birth of the second child.

The payments do not so much give stability to the union of marriage as they are a recognition of its stability. The parents do not accept a suitor unless they are satisfied that he has the qualities of a good husband; and I have shown how the marriage is slowly formed through a series of ceremonies and rites, each marking a stage in the transference of the wife from her own people to her husband's people. Each rite is an acknowledgement that the marriage is a little more stable and complete and compels further payments, which are both an expression on the part of the husband's people of a sense of security and a means of bringing about the next rite, and through it greater security. When the bride's people consent to hold the next ceremony they express by so doing their confidence in the final outcome. Marriage is not a single act. It is a succession of interconnected acts leading from courtship to the birth of children, and bridewealth is not a single payment but a succession of payments in response to the changing status of the wife and the increasing maturity of the union. As Nuer see it, these payments continue long after the marriage is fully established in the birth of calves and the progeny of these calves and of their progeny, a constant redocumentation which is balanced by the birth of children to the wife and of children to these children.

Bridewealth has so far been viewed as a means of organizing personal relations between the husband and his people on one side and the wife and her people on the other side. It has also a more general structural function. When a woman is married she is transferred from one lineage to another. The husband alone has sex rights in her, but all his brothers and paternal cousins have residual sex rights in her, and his unmarried brothers may benefit from her labour as much as he does. The husband's exclusive marital privilege is recognized in the acknowledgement that he may claim damages for adultery. He has, of course, also rights in any children she may bear, but the children are not only his. They are children of his lineage. The rights of the husband and any of his kin living with him to the domestic services of his wife are evident in the performance of them and in the acceptance that he may correct her should she neglect them.

For the loss of their daughter, or rather of her children, her lineage receive cattle which enable them to obtain a wife from a third lineage to bear them children. When the daughters of these wives are married, the cattle received for them enter the kraals of the lineages to replace those which left them on the marriages of their mothers. In practice the total operation is not as simple as I have stated it because the cattle do not all go to one lineage but are partly distributed among the kinsmen of the bride's father and mother, but this is corrected by the fact that the cattle the father and paternal uncles do not receive on the marriage of their daughter come to them through other marriages in which they stand to the bride in other relationships. Hence it is that Nuer often speak of the lineage marrying a wife with its cattle or giving their daughter in marriage to another lineage for cattle. They say, for example,

that '*cieng* Pual have married a wife', or that '*cieng* Dumien have
given their daughter in marriage'.

To understand the functions of bridewealth in Nuer society it
is therefore necessary to view its payment in a wider social setting
than is provided by any particular marriage. It is necessary to see
it, as Nuer themselves do, as a series of transactions, and to perceive furthermore in an exchange of cattle for a wife an exchange
of a daughter for a wife. Bridewealth may be fruitfully compared
from this point of view with bloodwealth, the payment of cattle in
compensation for homicide. This is forty head of cattle, the same
number as is paid for a bride, and the cattle are divided among the
kinsmen of the dead man on the same plan of distribution as that
obtaining in the distribution of bridewealth, though about half are
reserved for marrying a wife to the name of the dead man to bear
him a son. As bridewealth enables a woman to be replaced by a
woman so bloodwealth enables a man to be replaced by a man. It is
worthy of note that the rate of bloodwealth has fallen in recent
times to about the same level as the rate of bridewealth. Nuer see
the similarity between them, for I have heard them complain that
the government was attempting to fix bloodwealth without fixing
bridewealth at the same rate, whereas what the one is the other
should be.

To see the Nuer custom of bridewealth in its structural per-
spective we must therefore think in terms of lineages. Children
are attached by payment of bridewealth to the lineage of their
father. They are 'children of the cattle' and therefore of the man
in whose name they were paid, and they become joints in his
branch of descent. The man in whose name the cattle were paid
is always their pater, the legal or lineage father, whether he is their
genitor or not. If he dies, the widow should be taken by one of her
'husbands' and the 'fathers' of his sons, that is to say, by one of his
brothers. But even should a widow decline to cohabit with one of
her husband's paternal kin and prefer to live as a concubine with
some man unrelated to her dead husband, any children she may
bear are his children. Every child must have a pater or, which is
saying the same thing among the Nuer, belong to a lineage, and if
an unmarried woman has a child it is legitimatized either by sub-
sequent payment of bridewealth or by payment of a fee.

The two most important functions of bridewealth in Nuer
society appear to me, therefore, to be its role in creating new social

ties between persons and of regulating the interrelations between these persons till such time as their relationships become assimilated to kinship patterns—broadly speaking its role in the kinship system—and its structural role in interlineage relations.

V

The parents and kin of a young wife scarcely acknowledge her husband's existence until a second child has been born to the union. If there is any need to refer to him they speak of him as *co*, the husband of, followed by his wife's name, and they speak of his village as his wife's village and of his children by reference to her name and not to his. It is also customary for the wife's people to give her children different personal names from those given them by their father's people, and if they address them by an honorific title they use that of their own clan and not that of the husband's clan.

Nevertheless, after the birth of the first child the marriage is held to have become a complete union. The husband has established a kinship tie with his wife's kin, who now address him as father of so-and-so, after the name of his eldest child. He is no longer merely the husband of their daughter. Instead of paying clandestine visits to the home of his parents-in-law (*ciengthu*) he may visit them openly, though he must continue to treat his in-laws, particularly his parents-in-law, with great respect, expressed in formal modes of address, which are reciprocal, and in other ways, most emphatically in the prohibitions on eating in their home and appearing naked before them.

Even before a young man has started to look for a bride he will not generally eat with much senior men, unless they are kin, because one of them might become his father-in-law. Once he has asked for a girl's hand in marriage he may in no circumstances eat in her home, and the prohibition continues, sometimes greatly to his discomfort, until two or three children have been born, when it is relaxed by a formal ceremony if the parties are on good terms with one another. The father-in-law prepares beer, kills a goat or sheep, and invites the son-in-law and his kin to his home to partake of a feast. He tells his son-in-law that there is no need for him to respect his parents-in-law any more. The son-in-law will refuse to eat, however, till compelled to do so by the insistence of his father-in-law's kin and by his father-in-law's gift of a cow, 'the cow of the eating of the husband of a daughter', to *cocangnyade*, his daughter's husband's brother. This ceremony is sometimes held when a young sister of the wife is about to be married, so that her husband may take part in the nuptial feasts. Later, the father-in-law visits the homestead of his daughter's husband's brother and will be given beer and meat. Before he can eat or drink he must be given a bull calf or sheep by the owner of the homestead. His daughter's husband is now said to regard him as a father. Before these payments have been made, a son-in-law is to his father-in-law and his wife's paternal uncles in a position formally like that of the kin of a slayer to the kin of the man he has slain in that they cannot eat in one another's homes. The maternal uncle of a wife, who is also *gwanthu*, his father-in-law, may likewise give her husband's brother a goat to enable the husband to eat in the homes of his wife's maternal kinsmen.

A son-in-law also respects his parents-in-law by hiding his naked-ness in their presence with a wild cat's skin from the day he asks for their daughter's hand in marriage till the day his brother receives a cow to enable him to eat in their home. While the prohibition is in force a son-in-law who is living in the same village or camp as his parents-in-law avoids them as far as possible even when he is wearing a skin. A son-in-law must also—at any rate in some parts of Nuerland—wear sandals when visiting his mother-in-law, as he is dangerous to her should he visit her bare-footed and might cause her to become barren. There are various other customs indi-cating the mother-in-law to son-in-law relationship, such as the obligation on the survivor, should either die, to visit the grave a few days after burial and throw a bracelet on it. Also a son-in-law must not visit his parents-in-law when they are sick, and they must not visit him when he is sick. A man avoids his mother-in-law and her attitude to him is one of shyness and reserve. Unlike fathers-in-law and brothers-in-law, who ask a husband directly for whatever they want, a mother-in-law trusts that her son-in-law will remem-ber her wants or, if in great need, asks him for a gift through her daughter. The mother-in-law relationship among the Nuer is a subject of mirth, and the foulest slips of the tongue are attributed to mothers-in-law when talking to their daughters' husbands.

All these rules regulating the behaviour of a man to his parents-in-law, and the avoidance and the attitude of reserve which accom-pany them, are eased after the birth of a second child and slowly break down as patterns of affinity change into patterns of kinship, the husband becoming 'the father of our daughter's children' instead of 'our daughter's husband'. A man may even joke with his mother-in-law when there are several children.

The rules about eating and nakedness apply, though in a lesser degree, to kinsfolk of the wife of her parents' generation as well as to the parents themselves, for all her kinsfolk are her husband's in-laws. A man will not appear naked or eat in the homes of his wife's paternal and maternal uncles and aunts or appear naked before the wives of his wife's close kinsmen. I have seen a man's wife's paternal aunt make a great fuss when unintentionally he appeared naked before her. He knelt behind another man to hide his nakedness and receive her reproaches when he became aware of his misdemeanour. On another occasion the fuss was made by a bride's paternal uncle's wife while the astonished bridegroom hastily retired into a hut. Unintentional affronts of this kind are quieted by small payments, such as a spear or a goat. As the genealogical distance from the wife increases, the obligation on the part of her husband to observe these rules lessens. It altogether ceases when the wife's father and maternal uncle have paid beasts to enable him to eat in their homes. Should a divorce take place, the son-in-law at once ceases to treat his in-laws with respect.

The wife's brother and her other kinsmen of his generation are not avoided, but her eldest brother may refrain from eating with the bridegroom before a child has been born. Nuer say, 'the wife's brother is your brother; since he gave you his sister he became your brother', and 'the husband of your sister is your brother because he will get a cow (the *yang waca*) on the marriage of your daughter'. After the birth of children a man and his wife's brother can, if great friends, jokingly curse one another in obscene language. The wife's brother's wife is highly respected till a child has been born, though not to the same extent as the mother-in-law, unless the mother-in-law is dead; then 'she becomes your mother-in-law and must be respected as deeply as a mother-in-law'. Nuer say that she then becomes your real mother-in-law and that '*ca mandong*', 'she has become a grandmother' (to the children of her husband's sister, who call their maternal uncle's wife 'grand-mother'). The only in-law whom a man need not at any time treat with reserve is his wife's sister. He can joke with her and even exchange abusive language with her. However, if his mother-in-law is dead he treats her eldest daughter with reserve, for she has then taken her mother's place: 'she has placed the food on the fire' (at her mother's mortuary ceremony). A man and his wife's sister's husband, whom he calls *warombaida*, may be on intimate terms.

It is only when the bride is still a maiden that the father and uncles and brothers of the bridegroom are reserved with his parents-in-law. After the marriage is consummated only the husband's father or, if the father is dead, his eldest brother will respect his parents-in-law and only to a small extent, not usually with regard to nakedness and food. Nevertheless, it is customary for the father of the bridegroom to give the father of the bride a spear or goat, and for the father of the bride to make him a similar gift, to enable the two men to eat in one another's homes without shame. A husband's younger brothers do not in any way respect his inlaws and they eat and go naked in their homesteads. On the other hand, it is customary, at any rate in the Lou tribal area, for the youth who acted as the husband's best man in the marriage ceremonies to respect his in-laws till they give him a goat to break down his reserve.

Obviously a wife is in a different position *vis-à-vis* her husband's people from that of a husband *vis-à-vis* his wife's people. Nevertheless, while avoidance is impracticable, she treats her parents-in-law with great respect, and in the early days of her marriage she keeps herself apart from them as much as domestic requirements permit. She cannot eat with her mother-in-law, and this prohibition may continue for some years after the birth of her first child. She cannot eat in her husband's home at all before the birth of her first child, and even after this event, when she has come to live with him, she ought not to see him eat or be seen eating by him. However, the inconvenience of this prohibition is evident, and soon after she has taken up residence in her husband's home it will be arranged that her husband enters as though by accident a hut in which she is eating. After this it is no longer shameful for husband and wife to see one another eating, and though the wife is at first shy, she will eventually share her husband's meal when they are alone. Before the birth of her first child a woman respects her husband's sisters and will not eat out of the same dish with them. After the birth of a child she can be on free and easy terms with them, though personal difficulties sometimes make for reserve. Should the mother be dead, her eldest daughter tends to take her place in the family, and this affects her relationship to her brother's wife.

Just as a husband need not respect his wife's sisters but is on familiar terms with them, so a wife is on familiar terms with her husband's brothers. Among brothers the wife of one is in a general social sense the wife of all. A man seldom refers to his brother's wife as '*ciekdemar*', 'the wife of my brother', but as '*ciekgoala*', 'the wife of my home', and she refers to him as '*gwangaanko*', 'the father of our children.' Another word a wife uses to refer to her husband's brothers (mostly for his younger brothers), and also for his paternal cousins, is '*cocangda*', which seems to mean 'my husband of the daytime' as distinct from the husband of the night, the real husband, for Nuer say that '*corar gule, cowar gule*', 'the husband of the outside is different, the husband of the night is different'.* Here again, though relations between a wife and her husband's brothers are free and easy, should her father-in-law be dead the eldest brother takes his place as head of the family and must be treated with deference. When she has borne several children she and her husband's brothers and paternal cousins may curse each other in foul language. In the horseplay which takes place on the day boys are initiated and on the day initiates pass out of seclusion it is the *cocangda*, generally a paternal cousin of the husband, who lifts up the skirt of the mother of an initiate and spits and utters a cry.

A woman enters her husband's home as a wife of the home. She also enters it as the mother of a child of her husband's lineage, and this is emphasized by the usual teknonymous mode of address for a married woman in her husband's community—mother of so-and-so, after the name of her eldest child, the link which joins her to her husband's lineage—in contrast to the patronymic mode of address for the husband—son of so-and-so, after the name of his father, his link with his lineage. Through the child she has kinship with the people of the home of her adoption by marriage. '*Jigoala*', 'people of my home', a woman's favourite ejaculation, is the term by which she refers collectively to the domestic society of which she regards herself as a member. The expression was constantly on her lips before marriage in reference to her paternal family and kin. When she comes to live with her husband it is still constantly

* However, Father Kiggen (*Nuer–English Dictionary*, 1948, p. 63) gives *couciang*, a formation which would not bear the same literal meaning as *cocang*.

on her lips, but then it means the people of her husband's home, for they have become her people, and she now identifies herself with them and not with her father's people. She uses in speaking to her husband's kin the same terms of address as he uses.

When a woman joins her husband she comes under the protection of his lineage spirits and ancestral ghosts, and when she builds a mud windscreen they are summoned by her husband's father to come and abide there. On the day she constructs it her father-in-law pours over it beer and butter and utters some of the pious formulae spoken on such occasions. When beer is brewed the wife pours a little at the side of the windscreen, and a sacrificial goat or sheep is often tethered there for the ghosts to see it before it is killed. When the woman who owns the hut has a grandchild, a *gat-nyade*, a son of her daughter, she sends for the boy to come and break down her windscreen and sacrifice a goat. Since a wife is accepted by the ghosts and spirits of her husband's lineage, she may perform ritual for that lineage in which invocation of its ghosts and spirits forms part.

But though a woman joins her husband's group and becomes part of it, she never entirely ceases to belong to her own family and lineage, under the protection of whose ghosts and spirits she remains. If she is ill treated by her husband she will ask her father and uncles and brothers to help her. On the other hand, should she in a quarrel with her husband disfigure him—knock a tooth out, for example—her father must pay him compensation. I have myself on two occasions seen a father pay a heifer to his son-in-law to atone for insults hurled at the husband's head by his wife when irritated by accusations of adultery.

I have given a short account of the conventional attitudes and patterns of behaviour Nuer regard as proper between relations-in-law. I repeat that for Nuer the relationships which contain these attitudes and patterns change in course of time into a kind of kin-relationship through the children to the marriage, and they might then perhaps be best described as kinship-in-law.

VI

So far I have been speaking about normal matrimony, the usual domestic union in Nuer society. There are, however, other forms of domestic union among the Nuer of which I now give an account.

I presented in Chapter I some genealogical tables to illustrate

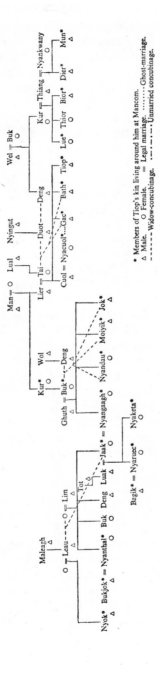

* Members of Tiop's kin living around him at Mancom.
△ Male. ○ Female. = Legal marriage. .... Ghost-marriage.
----- Widow-concubinage. .—.—. Unmarried concubinage.

the network of kinship ties we find in any local community of Nuerland. Though these tables were simplified, they showed some of the different domestic unions which I am about to describe. Before doing so, and in order that their significance in the networks of kinship ties to which I have referred may be better appreciated, I subject another configuration of kin to the scrutiny of a more powerful lens than that used in the examination of the earlier specimens. The diagram above, and a brief commentary on it, reveal some of the complications these forms of union make in kinship relations. The people figured in it were living in 1935 in the Eastern Jikany village of Mancom, a large settlement, containing a high proportion of persons of Dinka descent, at the mouth of the Nyanding river. I spent over a month there in the rains of that year because it was the home of Tiop-Lier, a youth whom I knew well and who was at the time acting as my cook. His relatives made me welcome on his account.

I made an investigation into the kinship structure of the village, but I purpose here only to give a brief account of Tiop's own home, the immediate companions of his daily life. Lier, Tiop's pater, was a Luac Dinka. He married Tai, who bore him a son Cuol, who died from the bite of a snake while still a boy. After her husband's death Tai went to live with a man called Duot. Duot and Lier are known to have been distantly related through their mothers, being *ram kene gatmanlen*, a man and his mother's sister's son (in a classificatory sense), but Tiop and his brothers were unable to trace the relationship between them with genealogical precision. By Duot, Tai bore two sons, Gac and Bath. Between the births, however, Tai had a disagreement with her lover and went to live for a time with a man called Deng-Wel, at present living in the interior of Lou country, by whom she bore my friend Tiop. Gac, the eldest of the three brothers, had recently married a wife, Nyacuol, to the name of his dead paternal half-brother Cuol. It had been arranged that when Bath marries he is to take a wife to the name of his dead genitor Duot.

Tiop, through whose eyes I saw the social world around us at Mancom, had come to live there to be near his natural *wac*, his genitor's sister, Kur (since dead) and her sons, and in 1935 he and his brother Bath were sharing a byre with Dier and Mun, the sons of her co-wife. Tiop and Bath called these youths '*gaatwacda*', 'sons of my paternal aunt', and they called Tiop and Bath '*gaatnara*', 'sons of my maternal uncle', though in the usual Nuer fashion they all addressed each other as '*demar*', 'my mother's son'. Later Tiop brought to live at Mancom his legal *wac*, his pater's sister, also called Kur, from Lak tribal country. This Kur had a daughter called Buk who had married a husband, Ghuth, and had borne him a daughter, Nyangaagh, before leaving him on account of ill treatment to go to live in the country of the Luac Dinka from which her mother's people had originally come. There she lived as concubine to Deng Wol, to whom she bore a daughter and two sons. All efforts by her husband to secure her return failed, and though he seized Nyangaagh and brought her back to his home she ran away and returned to her mother. Later, in a year of famine, Tiop's brother Gac brought Kur and her daughter Buk and Buk's children to live at Mancom. Ghuth contented himself by taking the cattle on the father's side on the marriages of Buk's daughters.

The eldest of them, Nyangaagh, was married by a woman, Jaak-Lim, to the name of her dead brother. The father of Jaak-Lim had two daughters at the time of his death, Buk and Nyanthal. His widow became concubine to Leau-Maleagh, to whom she bore a third daughter Jaak who, as already stated, married Nyangaagh, Tiop's *nyanyawac*, paternal aunt's daughter's daughter. Jaak had herself been previously married to Luak-Tot and had borne him two children before his death. She called in Nyok, the son of her genitor, to give her, or rather to give her dead brother, children by Nyangaagh.

It will thus be seen that to Tiop and his brothers the immediate and intimate circle of kinsmen among whom they live and share their daily experience are the clusters of kin around their paternal aunt Kur and Tiop's natural paternal aunt of the same name. It is for this reason that in giving me the connexions of his family Tiop always stressed the female links which united him to those around him and neglected the names of the husbands of these women, for they had little interest for him.

The genealogical chart of Tiop's immediate social milieu contains examples of several different types of union other than matrimony in the ordinary sense, ghost-marriage, widow-concubinage, woman-marriage, and a variety of unmarried concubinage, and will serve as a starting-point for an examination of these diverse unions which have so important a place in the social life of the Nuer.

The ordinary Nuer marriage is a union such as we understand matrimony to be in our own civilization, with this difference perhaps, that the Nuer do not consider the union to be complete till a child is born to it. As we have seen, a Nuer union of this kind is instituted by payment of cattle and the performance of nuptial ceremonies. It is to this type of union that I refer when I speak of marriage without qualifications; and when I use the word family in an unqualified sense I refer to the partners to such a union and the children born to the wife in the union (but not necessarily begotten by the husband). However, since the terms marriage and family are also used in this book in a qualified sense to refer to other unions and groups, I sometimes speak of a simple legal marriage and a simple legal family to avoid confusion or to point a contrast.

When a man marries two or more women there results a complex legal family, which we call a polygamous family, in which are comprised several simple legal marriages with the male partner the same in all of them. I discuss some of the features of polygamous marriages and families in the following chapter. They present no immediate difficulties.

What seems to us, but not at all to Nuer, a somewhat strange union is that in which a woman marries another woman and counts as the pater of the children born of the wife. Such marriages are by no means uncommon in Nuerland, and they must be regarded as a form of simple legal marriage, for the woman-husband marries her wife in exactly the same way as a man marries a woman. When the marriage rites have been completed the husband gets a male kinsman or friend or neighbour, sometimes a poor Dinka, to beget children by her wife and to assist, regularly or when assistance is particularly required, in those tasks of the home for the carrying out of which a man is necessary. When the daughters of the marriage are married he will receive for each a 'cow of the begetting' and more beasts if he has played any considerable part in the maintenance of the home. We may perhaps refer to this kind of union as woman-marriage.

A woman who marries in this way is generally barren, and for this reason counts in some respects as a man. She acquires cattle through the marriages of kinswomen, including some of those due to uncles on the marriage of a niece, or by inheritance, since she counts as a man in these matters. A barren woman also often

(108)

practises as a magician or diviner and thereby acquires further cattle; and if she is rich she may marry several wives. She is their legal husband and can demand damages if they have relations with men without her consent. She is also the pater of their children, and on the marriages of their daughters she receives 'the cattle of the father', and her brothers and sisters receive the other cattle which go to the father's side in the distribution of bridewealth. Her children are called after her, as though she were a man, and I was told that they address her as 'father'. She administers her home and herd as a man would do, being treated by her wives and children with the deference they would show to a male husband and father.

A very common feature of Nuer social life is a union I have called ghost-marriage. If a man dies without legal male heirs, a kinsman of his or the succeeding generation—brother, natural son, paternal nephew, or, where a man has, in the absence of lineal heirs, inherited cattle from his mother's brother, sister's son—ought to take a wife to his name.

Except in the case of a barren woman and in the special circumstances and manner mentioned on page 16, where it might be said that in a sense she does so, a daughter does not carry on the lineage of her father. She becomes one of her husband's people and her children belong to his lineage. Hence Nuer say: '*Nyal, mo ram me gwagh*', 'A daughter, that is an unrelated person.' As the Roman lawyers put it, she is *finis familiae*, the terminus of the family. But a man's name must continue in his lineage, and Nuer consider it very wrong if a man who dies without male heirs is not married a wife by a kinsman who will raise up seed to him by her so that he will be remembered in his sons. This is a most elementary obligation of kinship, and if it is neglected the dead man's ghost may haunt his kin.

In speaking of these ghost-marriages Nuer say, for example, that '*ce deman kwen ciek*', 'he–his brother–married–wife' ('he married his brother a wife'). This is a clumsy and ambiguous expression in English, so I shall speak of a man marrying a wife to the name of a dead kinsman, it being understood that it is not he, but the dead man, who is the legal husband. Nuer also speak of a man 'kindling the fire' of his dead kinsman, a euphemism for raising up seed to him.

This is a vicarious marriage, the vicarious husband acting as though he were the true husband in the marriage ceremonies and afterwards in cohabitation and domestic life. In all but the strict legal sense he counts as husband and father in the family. He has the same legal rights over the wife as her husband would have were he alive, and he exercises the same authority over the children when they are minors as their pater would do. While the children are small, at any rate, one cannot observe any difference in sentiment and behaviour between a ghost-family and a simple legal family. It is only when the sons grow up that their connexion with their pater becomes significant. In everyday usage people speak of the living man as though he were the true husband and father, so that it is only by inquiring that one discovers the name of the true husband. The name of the pater looms larger when the children grow up, and Nuer told me that it is his name which finally survives in the genealogy of the lineage; but when the pater and the genitor are agnatic kin it is by reference to the name of the genitor that the children will be addressed, except in certain legal and ceremonial situations when it is desired to indicate their correct genealogical position. A child always knows the name of his pater.

Nevertheless, the legal partners to the union are not the man and woman living together. The legal husband is the ghost in whose name the bridewealth was paid and the ritual of matrimony was performed. The woman is *ciekjooka*, the wife of a ghost, and her children are *gaatjooka*, children of a ghost. The family that develops out of a ghost-marriage may be called a ghost-family in acknowledgement of the ghostly status of the pater of the children. It consists of a ghost, his wife, his children born in the union of marriage, and the kinsman who begat these children and acts as father to them. It is a variety of the simple legal family, which is contained in its structure. This is why, Nuer say, a man may not marry a wife to the name of a kinsman of a younger generation, for such a marriage would mean that the wife would cohabit with a man who was her father-in-law.

These ghost-marriages must be almost as numerous as simple legal marriages. Not only do many youths die before marriage but for one reason or another married men do not always have male heirs. A man's wife may bear him only daughters or her sons may die before marriage. In this last eventuality, his kinsmen must raise up seed not only to him but to his sons also, unless they died in childhood. A very common circumstance is that a man takes a wife to the name of a dead kinsman and is unable later to marry a wife in his own right, for, seeing that he enjoys the material benefits of marriage, his younger brothers must be allowed to marry from the family herd before he can contract a second, and legal, marriage. If he is ever rich enough to marry again he may feel that he must forgo the privilege in the interests of the sons he has raised up to his dead kinsman. He thus dies legally childless and it will be the duty of one of these sons to marry a wife to his name. In a case of this kind, it is more than ever incumbent on his sons to marry a wife to his name because he has died in possession of cattle. These cattle, *ghok jookni*, cattle of the ghosts, are sacred and in the special circumstances ought not to be used for any purpose other than marrying a wife to the name of their dead owner. When Nuer raid a herd to seize cattle in compensation for some injury they will not take cattle reserved for the marriage of a ghost.

Except in the circumstances I have just related, it is usually a younger brother who marries a wife to the dead. As brothers marry in order of seniority, it is fitting that when it comes to the turn of the dead man to take a wife the brother next junior to him should marry in his name. However, if the next brother is only a paternal half-brother they are likely to leave the pious obligation to a full brother who is yet younger.

The custom of marrying a wife to the name of a dead man makes obvious complications in the kinship system of the Nuer, for a child of the union is both a son of the man who is in the place of his pater and, in virtue of his attachment to his pater, stands also to him in a different relationship: father's brother's son, brother, brother's son, or maternal uncle's son.

A further complication arises when, as occasionally happens, a woman marries a wife to the name of a dead kinsman, usually of a dead uterine brother. It is said: '*Ce rode kwen ciek, ciek thok dwiel man*', 'She has taken a wife to herself, a wife for the hut of her mother', that is to say, for her uterine brother. The persons involved in a marriage of this kind are the dead man, his kinswoman who marries a wife to his name, the wife, and the man who is brought in to cohabit with the wife. A woman may instead marry a wife herself and instruct the son of this marriage to marry a wife, when he grows up, for her brother (his paternal uncle, since the sister is his pater).

(111)

Yet more rarely a man marries a wife to the name of a dead sister or other kinswoman who was barren in her life, 'for she then counts as a man'. This is perhaps only done when the dead woman's ghost causes sickness to draw attention to her unhappy condition. The children are called after their female pater, and her brother, who has married their mother to her name, counts as their paternal uncle, 'for his sister has become his brother'. On the marriage of the daughters he gets the cattle due to a paternal uncle. It seems that he must not cohabit with the wife himself, because in these circumstances 'your wife is like your sister' (she stands in the place of your sister), but must arrange for a stranger, perhaps a Dinka, to cohabit with her in the hut he builds for her in his homestead.

Another type of union, and one that might be expected in a society which has ghost-marriage, is the levirate. Among many African peoples a widow is inherited by her dead husband's brother or son and becomes his wife. This is not the case among the Nuer. With them the bonds of marriage are not severed at death. The widow remains the wife of her dead husband, and any children she may bear after his death, by whomsoever they are begotten, count as his children. Hence Nuer never allow one to use the word *kwen*, to marry, in reference to the taking of a deceased brother's wife. They themselves usually say of the brother that *'ce ciekdeman lath dwil'*, 'he has provided his brother's wife with a hut'. She is still the wife of her dead husband and therefore cannot be remarried. Indeed, I found great difficulty in making the Nuer understand that in our country it is possible for a widow to remarry.

The levir is normally a brother, and a brother is the most approved substitute for the dead man. If a young man dies his sons would not be old enough to take his widow, and he is most unlikely in any case to have another wife than their mother. When an old man with several wives dies, the wives, being as a rule senior women, may be past child-bearing and therefore wish to live with their children, or they may prefer to lead an independent life with lovers than to live with a kinsman of the husband. It is only when an old man dies who has lately married a young wife, who has not yet borne a child or has borne a single child, that a son takes his father's wife. By this time all the father's brothers will have married; and it was probably understood at the time of the old

VI. A married woman, wearing skirt
In the background a man plays on a harp

man's marriage that he was taking the girl to wife for one of his sons. It is certainly rare today for a son to take his father's wife. I was told also that it very occasionally happens that a sister's son takes his mother's brother's widow. Sometimes a paternal cousin of some degree takes the widow. This may be regarded as coming within the idea of the levirate, and Nuer so speak of it. But it rarely happens, and when it happens the union, in fact, partakes more of the nature of concubinage than of leviratic marriage. A brother, especially a full brother, ought to be the levir, and if any of the brothers are unmarried their rights are paramount. So, bearing in mind these rare exceptions, we may use the term levirate in its classical sense.

Leviratic marriage is very different from ghost-marriage. In a ghost-marriage the vicarious husband actually marries the wife in the sense that he pays the cattle and performs the rites of marriage, even though in the name of another. In leviratic marriage the legal husband has performed these actions himself and the brother merely enters as pro-husband a family already in being. The widow is always referred to as the wife of the dead man and not as the pro-husband's wife, as she generally is in ghost-marriage. Moreover, the children clearly regard themselves as members of a legal family to which the brother of their pater does not belong, although he is their foster-father and may also be their genitor. He may be opposed by the sons when they grow up.

It is true that the brother is the accepted guardian of his dead brother's children, and if he enters into a leviratic union with the widow he has in it the status of legal representative of the husband, so that he can demand compensation if anyone commits adultery with her. He can also, in certain circumstances, as I will explain, divorce her. To this extent leviratic marriage must be regarded as a variety of legal marriage, the simple legal family being contained in its structure as it is in the structure of the ghost-family. But it is also true that, in practice, the pro-husband in leviratic marriage has far less control over his partner than the pro-husband in ghost-marriage; and a widow in Nuer leviratic marriage is much freer than an inherited widow in other African societies. Her favourable position is due to the rule by which a widow is still married to her dead husband, for after his death she can continue to perform her reproductive obligations to his lineage by bearing him children as well by a stranger as by one of his brothers, and as well in the home of a stranger as in the home of her husband's kin. If she has children begotten by her husband, her domestic duties to her husband's people are adequately performed by her services to his children. In these circumstances the husband's kin must give her her freedom.

Briefly, the position is this. A woman is married not simply by her husband but by his brothers as well, since she is married with the cattle of their common herd. Consequently, if her husband dies, his brothers expect to exercise their rights in her, and if she is young and some of the brothers are unmarried they may insist on them to the point of dissolving the marriage if they are denied them. In practice, a young widow generally consents to live with one of her husband's younger unmarried brothers. Tradition, good form, and the threat of divorce are powerful sanctions to conformity in this matter, though these influences are not so strong in the case of a paternal half-brother as in the case of a full brother. After the death of a man the children of each of his wives often live with their mothers as largely independent units, each mother looking after the home of her children. If the mother is dead and the eldest son of the hut is married, his younger brothers and his unmarried sisters group themselves round his home, where his wife cooks for them and milks their cows. She takes the place of the mother. Unmarried youths are then dependent on the wife of a full brother for daily necessities, and if he dies and she does not consent to live with one of them, they lose not only a mate but also a housekeeper, cook, dairy-maid, and gardener. They therefore strongly object to her going to live with a lover, especially a lover in a different village. If they are on good terms with their half-brothers they will not resist the widow's desire to live with one of them, but will group themselves around the half-brother whom she chooses, and share his byre and the domestic services of their dead brother's wife in his homestead. If they are not on good terms with their half-brothers they may out of spite tell her, if she refuses to live with one of themselves, to go and bear children by a stranger. Much depends on the strength of family sentiment in any particular case. A full brother has strongest claims on the widow and the strongest feelings of obligation to the dead and his family, and he is therefore likely to oppose her, should she wish to take a lover, more strongly than half-brothers and paternal cousins would do, for their claims are weaker and they have less personal interest in the family of the dead, sometimes caring little with whom the widow lives so long as they get their shares of the bridewealth of her daughters.

One finds that, in practice, a young widow who has borne her husband a single child sometimes lives with strangers. The husband's kin try to persuade her to live with a brother, but if they fail, they often, especially in eastern Nuerland, reconcile themselves to her obduracy, though they may insist that she continues to live in their village, as a member of their home, and there bear children to her dead husband by a lover. If she refuses this stipulation they can divorce her, leaving with her parents six head of the bridewealth cattle to retain their rights in the child. If she agrees to it they have few grounds for complaint. The children she bears by a lover are not only their kin but they are born amidst them and reared by them, and the lover not only begets children for them but also acts as their protector and breadwinner if he is a member of the village, or frequently visits the mother to assist her in gardening if he lives in a neighbouring village.

The position of a widow who has borne her husband two or more children is different. The return of her bridewealth cannot in any case be demanded: '*Ghok te jokdien ka nath ca ka de lony*', 'Cattle which have people (children) on their backs cannot be loosened (returned).' In these circumstances a woman is free to live where and with whom she pleases, and in fact many Nuer widows of this seniority do not live with kinsmen of their dead husbands but 'give birth in the bush' ('*dieth dor*'), as the Nuer say. Wherever a widow lives and by whomsoever her children are begotten, they are all children of the dead husband and their kin will claim them sooner or later. When she is old and past child-bearing she will probably return to her husband's home to be with her grownup sons. A widow who has grown-up children at the time of her husband's death will not want to take a lover. She will choose to live with one of her children.

A widow is asked to make her choice at her husband's mortuary ceremony. The kin are not likely to challenge her decision on this solemn occasion. If she refuses the brothers and sons of her husband, they ask her whether she wishes to take a lover away from their village (*lum dor*) or to take a lover in the village (*lum cieng*). They hope that she will choose the latter alternative. However, widows often elect to return to their paternal homes and there take lovers, so that, as we have earlier noted, it often comes about that children are brought up among their maternal kin. Many widows neither remain for long in the homes of their dead husbands nor in the homes of their own kinsfolk, but after a while go to live with lovers, sometimes in different districts and even in different tribal areas. Relations between a widow and her lover tend to be unstable, and she often abandons one lover to take another. She may wander from place to place. If her children by her husband are small she takes them with her, so during childhood they are members of the households of her lovers, who act as their foster-fathers. Thus a widow may go to live with a lover accompanied by children begotten both by her husband and by former lovers. Some old widows, long past child-bearing, live with men to cook for them, the man having no wife and the widow no adult children to look after her.

When a widow lives with a man who is not of her husband's kin we have a different kind of union to that of leviratic marriage. Indeed, it cannot be regarded as marriage in any sense, but must be regarded as a form of concubinage. I call it widow-concubinage. A widow-concubine—that is to say, a widow who takes a stranger for a lover—is called in Nuer a *ciek ma lak*, and a child of such a union is called a *gat laka*, a child of concubinage. The structure of the original simple legal family remains unimpaired, however much the configuration of the household may change: it consists throughout of the wife, the husband who married her with cattle, and the children of the wife. Whoever begets these children, their pater is the husband of their mother. The *concubinus* does not stand in the place of the husband and has therefore no authority over the wife. He cannot compel her to live with him—she goes from man to man or has a succession of lovers in her own home as she feels inclined—and he has no redress if she has relations with other men while she is living with him. His position is thus very different from that of a man living in leviratic marriage. Likewise, he has no legal control over the children, who can be taken away from him by the kin of their pater whenever they choose to remove them. He is only their genitor, and his sole right in them lies in the obligation of their paternal kin to pay him a 'cow of the begetting' when each of his natural daughters by the widow is married. His position in this respect also is very different from that of a levir. A brother stands in the place of the pater, a lover does not. Consequently the group that results from the union of widow-concubinage, when children are born of it, must be regarded as a natural family and not, as in the cases we have hitherto been considering, a variant of the legal family.

There is another kind of domestic union to which I must allude in this place, because it corresponds to widow-concubinage in all respects but one: that the wife is not a widow. A man marries a wife who for some reason is not content to remain with him after she has borne him a child, and she leaves him. Her family are not prepared to pay back to the husband's people the cattle they have received from them, either because they cannot do so or because they consider that the breach is the husband's fault and not their responsibility. They tell the husband to let their daughter bear him children 'in the bush'. He may then have to acquiesce in his wife living with another man in some distant village. He is in any case the pater of any children she may bear to other men. She is still his wife, since his cattle are 'on her back', but nevertheless he cannot claim compensation for adultery, for she is living apart from him in circumstances which may not have his approval but which he has perforce to accept. The union between his wife and her lover can be classed as a variety of widow-concubinage, though Nuer tend to speak of her as a simple concubine.

In all the forms of union I have so far described—simple legal marriage, woman-marriage, ghost-marriage, leviratic marriage, and widow-concubinage—the woman is always legally married and all her children belong in virtue of her marriage to her husband's lineage. I now describe a type of union in which the mother is not married to any man, and which may perhaps be called unmarried concubinage or simple concubinage. A girl is dissatisfied with the man to whom she has been espoused and provokes a divorce, if such it can be called, before she has borne a child. This may happen a second time with a second husband, and her parents, finding that they cannot control their daughter, let her do as she pleases. This may mean allowing her to live with a man of whom she is fond but who cannot, or will not, marry her with cattle. Other women of this category are those who have borne children while maidens and have never afterwards been married. An unmarried concubine is called by Nuer a *ciek ma keagh*, and a child by her is known as a *gat keaka*. Their definition of her status is that 'she has no cattle on her back'. 'A *keagh* is a woman from whose back cattle have been returned.' Either the cattle paid for her have been sent back to her husband's people or she was not at any time married with cattle. These concubines often spend a few years with one lover and then a few years with another. They move from village to village, taking their infants with them. I found unmarried mothers in every Nuer village where I made inquiries; and I have known an unmarried concubine bear eight children by as many as seven different men.

Those unmarried concubines whom I have known personally have been women of strong character who valued their independence and did not desire matrimony. Nuer recognize that they are temperamentally unfit for normal married life and are unlikely to settle down till they are old. Their behaviour is not stigmatized as immoral, but they are not so highly esteemed as wives and in a quarrel their children may suffer the reproach of bastardy. Also, an unmarried concubine cannot expect the same support from her kinsmen in domestic disputes as a wife can expect. What a wife can demand as a right, a concubine can only ask as a privilege. It does not follow that a man treats a concubine differently to a wife, and one cannot know in a household who is wife and who is concubine by bare observation of behaviour. Indeed, a man may treat a concubine with more consideration than a wife, for he has only what control over her his personal influence gives him. He cannot claim compensation should she be unfaithful to him, and he cannot restrain her should she wish to leave him for a new lover.

He has, however, undisputed right to legitimatize any children she may bear him by paying for each child a fee of from four to six head of cattle to her parents—they are not divided among the kin. This fee (*ruok*) is not bridewealth. It gives him no rights in the woman nor in any further children she may bear to him or to other men. Children born of a concubine by different men become in consequence members of different lineages. If a concubine leaves one lover to live with another she takes her small children by the first with her to the second, but they will eventually be claimed by the man who by payment of cattle is their pater. By payment of a fee the genitor becomes the pater also.

It is, of course, possible for a man to legitimatize his union with a concubine by payment of bridewealth, but though he will almost invariably legitimatize his children, he is seldom eager to marry their mother, because experience has taught Nuer that a woman who leaves one man is likely to leave another. However, some women become concubines through misfortune, and not by choice, and are not unsuited or averse to the married state. A girl becomes pregnant in courtship and her swain has no cattle with which to marry her, or a young mother, unhappy when she comes to live in her husband's home, runs away from him and her bride-wealth is returned. In such circumstances a lover may well be pre-pared to pay bridewealth for her, though fewer cattle than he would pay for a maiden, and to go through the nuptial rites with her, so that he may have full legal rights in her and in all children she has borne or may bear to him or to any other man. The *ciek ma keagh*, unmarried concubine, then becomes *ciek pany*, a true wife. It sometimes happens too that a youth makes a girl pregnant and would like to marry her but has insufficient cattle. He pays what cattle he can get together, and the girl's people let him take her on the promise that he will pay the rest when he is able to do so; but they refuse to solemnize the marriage, so she is regarded as a sort of concubine. The marriage rites may not be performed till years afterwards, sometimes not till just before the marriage of her eldest daughter. Then the wedding dance is held and the cattle are blessed to make an honest woman of her, as we would say. Till then she can only be described as half-concubine, half-wife.

We may perhaps speak of an unmarried woman, the man with whom she lives, and the children she bears to him in his home as a simple natural family in contrast to a simple legal family. We cannot deny that this group is some kind of family, for its mem-bers live together in a common household on the pattern of a simple legal family, at any rate for some years. But whereas in the simple legal family the tie between pater and child is derived from the tie between husband and wife created by payment of bride-wealth, in the simple natural family it is a direct tie created by payment of cattle for the child and not for the mother. We may compare the simple natural family also with the kind of family that springs from widow-concubinage. This last is a complex group in that the woman and the children she bears to her lover belong not only to the natural family of a man, his mate, and their children, but to a different, and legal, family as well. The genitor can never pay a fee to become pater of his natural children. When a man begets children by an unmarried woman there is no legal family in opposition to this natural family and the genitor can become pater to the children. If the woman leaves him, his position is then equivalent to that of a man who has divorced his wife, but has left part of the bridewealth with her family to retain his children.

It is clear from the facts I have recorded that Nuer do not attach great importance to physiological paternity. Men prefer to beget their own sons, but it is not ignominious to nurture children begotten by others. Nuer pay little regard to the manner of begetting so long as the legal fatherhood of the child is well established. This is particularly evident in their ideas about adultery, and a consideration of them will serve also to emphasize that Nuer acknowledge social and mystical links between a child and his natural father.

It is adultery if a man has relations with another man's wife, including ghost-wives and leviratic wives. I was struck among the Nuer both by the frequency of adultery and the infrequency of quarrels or even talk about it. Nuer seem to treat the matter light-heartedly, and not to be at all ashamed of their adulteries. In speaking of adultery, it is the risk of being speared or clubbed if caught in the act, or having to pay compensation to the husband if he finds out what is happening, that they bring to the fore. Adultery in their eyes is an illegal but not an immoral act.

The legal position is as follows. When a husband has proof of his wife's infidelity he may claim compensation of six cows and, as the adulterer's kin are unlikely to support him, the husband will probably, if the two men live in the same district, receive the cattle. Nuer regard adultery in the husband's home as a more serious offence than adultery in the bush because they believe that it is more likely to cause the husband sickness. Adultery is a double damage: it is an infringement of rights and it can injure the husband's health.

If after the six head of cattle have been paid a healthy child is born of the adulterous congress, five of them must be returned, because 'the cattle and the child must not meet in one place'. Otherwise, the cattle paid in compensation partake of the nature of a legitimatization fee and hence give the genitor a claim on the child. The birth of a child seems to be thought to change the compensation for an adultery (*ruok*) into a fee for legitimatizing a child (also *ruok*). I only discovered this convention after I had left eastern Nuerland for good and was completing my study of the Nuer in western Nuerland, but Mr. Howell assures me that it is common to all the tribes to the east of the Nile except the Jikany. Among the western Nuer it is believed that if the cattle are not returned the child may die and his ghost haunt his pater. The sixth cow, the one that remains with the husband, is called *yang kula*, the cow of the hide. The payment protects the husband from the sickness he might otherwise suffer were he to have relations with his wife after the adulterer has had relations with her—on the same sleeping-hide, as the Nuer put it. Among the western Nuer an adulterer may even receive 'the cow of the begetting' on the marriage of a daughter born of his adultery. I was told that her kin do not relish paying it, but may do so because it is feared that otherwise he may curse her and cause her to be barren or her children to die in infancy. In no circumstances can an adulterer claim the child of his adultery. Likewise a youth who impregnates an unmarried girl cannot claim the child of his fornication.

It will have been noted that the test of the nature of a pro-creative union is in the division of the bridewealth of a daughter born of it among those who count in one or other way as members of her family, and I conclude this section by a summary of the rules which regulate its distribution. When the pater is alive he receives 'the cattle of the father' and 'the cattle of the mother'. If he is dead they go to his sons, the bride's full and half-brothers. In ghost-marriage and leviratic marriage these rights are vested in the bride's brothers. The genitor as such has no legal claim to these cattle, but, since in a ghost-marriage he stands in the place of the pater with regard to the bride's brothers as well as to the bride herself, the cattle in any case join his herd and he will dis-pose of them in the interests of his sons, the bride's brothers. When the genitor has begotten the bride in leviratic marriage, division of the cattle may be more complicated because the bride may have grown-up brothers begotten by her dead pater. When the bride has been born in widow-concubinage the cattle which are the right of the parents go to her brothers, those due to the father going particularly to any sons begotten by her pater.

The genitor in ghost-marriage and in leviratic marriage may always ask for a cow for having begotten the bride in addition to any cattle due to a kinsman standing in his relationship to her. 'The cow of the begetting' or 'the cow of the loins', as it is also called, is likewise paid to the genitor of daughters born in widow-concubinage, and if he acted also as foster-father to the bride and her brothers and sisters—'cut meat for them', as Nuer say—he may receive another two to four head of cattle of her bridewealth for having fostered the family. Also, when the daughter of his natural daughter is married, his legal son can claim a beast of the bridewealth. As I have explained, an adulterer may receive a cow on the marriage of his natural daughter, though I doubt if it is often paid.

There is no 'cow of the begetting' when the daughter of an unmarried concubine is married because the genitor by payment of a fee has made himself the pater also. 'The cattle of the father' go to him. As he is not the husband of the mother, 'the cattle of the mother', or some of them, may go to different kraals, because the bride's mother's sons have rights in them, and they may have been begotten and legitimatized by other men. For all these different cases I have stated only the principles of distribution of bridewealth. As I have explained earlier, actual distribution may be more complicated and depends on variable conditions. Among the Nuer these matters are discussed always in the idiom of cattle.

When a woman is married—that is to say, in all the cases we have considered except that of unmarried concubinage—division of the bridewealth of her daughters is determined by payment of bridewealth for herself. The person in whose name she was married with cattle is the pater of her children whether he begat them or not, was dead or alive at the time of her marriage and the birth of her children, or is a man or a woman. Hence it follows that agnatic descent is, by a kind of paradox, traced through the mother, for the rule is that in virtue of payment of bridewealth all who are born of her womb are children of her husband and therefore paternal kin, by whomsoever they may have been begotten. They may count as children of a man their mother has never even seen. They may have been begotten by several fathers, but they all have the same pater. It is the fertility of the womb which a lineage receives by payment of bridewealth. All children born of that womb belong to the lineage; they are all agnates. This is a profoundly significant fact in Nuer society. It affects, among other things, the position of the family group in the kinship and lineage systems. The custom by which men in ghost-marriage and leviratic marriage raise up seed to their kinsmen subordinates the exclusive interests of the family to those of the wider circles of the paternal kin and of the lineage. The prevalence of widow-concubinage and simple concubinage also strengthens sentiments of kinship, because there is in these cases no single undivided family, both legal and domestic, to demand a man's major allegiance at the expense of the solidarity of the wider kinship group which provides a boy with scope for his deepest interests and ambitions.

CHAPTER IV

THE FAMILY

I

SIMPLE legal marriage and the simple legal family which derives from it are standards to which the other kinds of union and family I have described are made to approximate in the interrelations of the persons concerned as far as circumstances permit. Even in widow-concubinage and in simple concubinage the male partner takes on himself, though to a lesser degree than a true husband, the attitude of respect a man should display to his parents-in-law. A man who lives with a woman and her children, whether as the legal representative of the husband and pater or not, models his relations with them on those obtaining in the home of a simple legal family. It is of such a home and family that I now give some account.

We noted in the first chapter that a Nuer homestead, the home of a family, to the household of which other kin may be attached, consists of a byre and its attendant hut or huts. The byre, a massive wattle-and-daub structure of some 15 to 20 feet in diameter, is the material and moral centre of the homestead. A man who builds a byre has started a family, herd, and home of his own. The byre stands for the father's status in the family. While he is alive his wives and sons and daughters are bound to him.

The byre looks on to the kraal and is the sleeping-place of the cattle in the rains; and some of the young men of the household may also sleep there, on a platform over the dung fire kept burning in the centre of it to give the cattle protection from mosquitoes. In the daytime it is the club-room of the household and the guest-room of the homestead, for byres, besides signifying the presence of a family and its head, are centres of social life in Nuer villages. When one sees a hut by itself it means that the byre has fallen down and has not yet been rebuilt or that the owner of the hut possesses at the time too few cattle to make it worth his while to build a byre for himself, since he can easily house his animals in that of a kinsman; unless it is the hut of an old widow or of a semi-detached concubine, neither of whom are likely to have cattle of their own. It sometimes happens that even an unmarried man may have a byre if he is the eldest son of a dead man. When he is initiated into manhood his paternal uncles ought to build him a byre, 'so that his father's fire may be relit', and to hand over to him his father's herd which they have held in trust till he should take his father's place as head of the family.

The wife has her hut at the side of the byre, and in a polygamous family each wife has her own hut, where she and her children sleep. Near to it there may be a simple shelter for cooking. In a large homestead there may also be a hut for the youths of the household to sleep in, and perhaps a hut for the senior girls. The head of the family has no hut of his own but sleeps in the huts of his wives. In such a polygamous family all the huts of the wives are built around the byre, and this attachment symbolizes for Nuer what we call the agnatic principle of their society, which insists that all the sons of a man belong to his lineage irrespective of their maternal affiliations, their links with the kin of their mothers through the different huts within the homestead. Very early in life small boys are driven by their father or elder brothers away from their mothers' huts to the byre, the place of the menfolk of the family, where they eat, sleep, and spend the leisure hours of the day. When they are about seven or eight years of age they sleep there instead of in their mothers' huts, where the women and girls eat and sleep and near which they spend most of the day. The men and boys, to whichever hut they may belong, belong also, and primarily, to the byre and to its *gol*, a word which means, as I have earlier explained, the fire of cattle-dung kept burning day and night in the centre of the byre (there is sometimes a second one in the kraal) and its hearth; and also homestead, hamlet, family, household, and even lineage in certain contexts. Daughters belong to the huts and they will be married from them into stranger lineages, into which they are absorbed. Sons belong to the byre and to the lineage of its owner. This connexion between byre and lineage is seen when a new byre is built, for then the master of ceremonies of the family is summoned to make a libation of beer to the guardian spirits and ancestral ghosts of the lineage before its central support is planted, so that they may give peace and prosperity to all who dwell therein. In the byre, at the side of the hearth, is kept a branch, decorated with metal rings and pieces of skins of sacrificed beasts, which serves as an ancestral shrine. In summer camps a windscreen takes the place

(125)

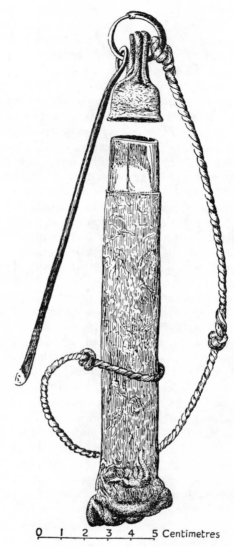

0   1   2   3   4   5 Centimetres

A snuff box
(Millet cane bound with the skin of a cow's tail)

of the byre as the men's dormitory and club, and the shrine is placed at its entrance. Small grass beehive huts take the place of the wattle-and-daub huts of the villages as the dwellings of the womenfolk of the home.

The polygamous family is a unit, the *gol* of the husband of the several wives. '*Jigoala*', 'the people of my hearth', are my family in this inclusive sense. But the children of each wife also belong exclusively to her *dwil* (or *ut*), hut, and to her *mac*, cooking-fire, so that the polygamous family is divided into a number of separate domestic groups within the larger whole. The huts of the different wives are the centres of these elementary families which have a common husband and father. Outside her hut each wife has her *buor*, a mud windscreen, against which she makes her cooking-fire, and near to it is her *thung*, a plastered hole in the ground for pounding millet (she has another fire-place and another pounding-hole inside her hut for use on rainy days). This mud screen, the top of which is fashioned into three humps, is the sign of a married woman's status as the mistress of her home and the mother of children, just as the hearth in the byre is the sign of a man's status as the father of a family and the master of household and herd; and it also has ritual associations, for sacrifices are made near it. It is the centre of a married woman's life. Here her friends and neighbours gossip with her when she is working or in the evening when work is done.

As boys grow up they attach themselves more and more to the byre, but each remains, both in sentiment and by social alinement, also a member of his mother's hut. Hence one may distinguish between full brothers and paternal half-brothers by saying that the first are brothers *kwi dwiel*, on the side of the hut (as we say, on the distaff side), while the second are brothers *kwi luak*, on the side of the byre (as we say, on the spear-side); and this distinction is a fundamental one in Nuer society, for it runs not only through the family but through the kin also, and is moreover the paradigm of the lineage structure.

With the huts go the gardens, with the byre go the cattle and the kraal. Each wife has her own garden and granaries, and with her millet she makes porridge for herself and her daughters, small sons, and guests, and also porridge and beer for the men and boys in the byre, the male members of the whole household, only some of whom would be her own sons, and any male neighbours and guests who may be present. A husband may have a garden of his own, but, if so, he distributes the millet among his wives when their supplies are running short.

The cattle belong to the husband. It is the usual practice for a man to divide his cows among his wives, but they only have the use of them for milking and cannot dispose of them. A cow given to a wife is merely what Nuer call 'a cow of the churning-gourd', seeing that it is given to the wife only so that she may have milk for her little ones and butter and cheese to pour over her porridge. It is true that the husband ought not to dispose of the cow without consulting her, and I have heard a wife protest strongly that she had not been advised of her husband's intentions; but she cannot refuse her consent to its disposal for the benefit of the family. Nor can she dispose of it herself. When I asked some Nuer whether a wife could give a cow which she always spoke about as 'my cow' to her brother, they wondered whether I was joking: 'Could she do such a thing? Would not her husband kill her? Give one of his cows to her brother indeed! Eh he!' If a man dies, leaving only young children, and his wives remain in his homestead or live with his brothers, they continue to have use of the cows he allocated to them during his lifetime. A dying man may expressly direct that they should do so. However, the trustees of the animals are the dead man's brothers and their disposal is subject to the claims of the family as a whole and must be in their common interest. If a widow tried to remove the cows from the herd and take them to the home of her brother, or of some man with whom she was living in concubinage, her husband's kin would certainly not, except in very special circumstances, permit their dispersal, for the cattle belong to the lineage, to the sons as a whole, who are links between the ancestors and its as yet unborn members. If the sons are men when their father dies they ought to go on living together round a common kraal. Nevertheless, as will be seen, they frequently do not do so. Whether they do so or not, the cattle belong to all of them and should be used, when the herd is large enough, to obtain wives for them in order of seniority, though in practice they are sometimes a bone of contention. Even cattle which come to wives on the marriages of their kinswomen (the cow of the paternal aunt and the cow of the maternal aunt) are not their property in an absolute sense. They have the use of them and should their husband die their sons inherit them, but while the

VII. A youth singing in praise of his ox. His arms are raised in imitation of its horns

husband is alive the beasts count as part of his herd and the wives
cannot dispose of them without his consent, which he can withhold. With the consent of the wife concerned, which she would
find it difficult to withhold, he can dispose of them for marriages
or other purposes.

A man also gives oxen to his sons so that they may display themselves in their company, but, here again, the sons do not have
rights in them against their father, who can use the animals for
any purpose he thinks fit, including the marriages of other sons
than those to whom he has given the beasts, though he would
promise a son deprived of his ox to replace it as soon as he could
do so. The only cattle a father cannot, or at any rate ought not to,
take for his own use without his sons' consent are those which
come to them by inheritance, for these are *ghok jookni*, cattle of
the ghosts. They may come through a dead mother's right, or the
son may be the child of a ghost-marriage or a leviratic marriage
and have a right to the herd of his pater, which should not be set
aside by the man who is acting in his father's place.

The family is an economic unit. Its members, with aid in certain undertakings from kinsmen and neighbours, maintain themselves and provide for their daily needs. None of the broader
departments of economy are exclusively the domain of either sex
and there is often direct mutual assistance between the sexes in the
performance of tasks. Also, tasks which are normally performed
by one sex may be performed by the other in circumstances which
render this necessary. Nevertheless, there is a clear, and complementary, division of labour between men and women. Boys'
work is mostly within the sphere of men's activities, the older boys
performing many adult tasks, and, except for milking, they take
no part in labour which is never done by men. Girls have the same
duties as women, to the extent their age permits.

Most of the labour connected with the flocks and herds falls to
the men and boys. The work of gardens is shared equally between
men and women, sons assisting their mothers and the husband
his wives. Only men hunt, and they and the boys do by far the
greater part of the fishing. Women collect wild fruits and roots.
Men do most of the building and repair of byres and huts, though
women do some of the lighter tasks in these activities. Most of the
daily tasks of the home, especially the preparation of food by
churning, pounding, grinding, cooking, and brewing, are the

exclusive privilege of women. Men manufacture most of the weapons and ornaments they use for themselves and for the cattle, and women the utensils and ornaments they use.

In general it may be said that men take on themselves a fair share of the labour of the home, that the routine work of the homestead is chiefly in the hands of women and a man's work very largely in the bush, and that tasks requiring greater strength are done by men. Division of labour between age-grades is also equitable.

A Nuer home is run by the combined efforts of all its members and the labour of running it is fairly distributed among them. One cannot but be struck by the camaraderie of the family as they assist one another in daily and seasonal tasks, either by direct aid or by co-ordination of activities. No work is considered degrading, no one is a drudge, all have leisure for rest and recreation, and all are content with their roles in the economy of the home. Indeed, the division of labour between sexes and ages accords with the social and personal freedom of women and children in Nuerland and with the recognition, so striking among the Nuer, of the independence and dignity of the individual.

I have omitted details in this brief account of division of labour, but there is one to which attention must be drawn. No man may milk the cows. This can only be done by women and uninitiated boys, and boys do not generally milk if there are women in the home. Woman's exclusive role of milkmaid combined with her roles of dairymaid and cook make her the centre of family and household. However many cattle a man may possess, he is helpless without a wife or mother or sister to milk the cows. It is only through marriage that a man can have a home of his own, and one of the most serious consequences of divorce is that it compels him to attach himself to the home of a kinsman whose womenfolk can milk and cook for him. Hence, also, if a man dies leaving motherless unmarried sons, efforts are made for the eldest of them to be married as soon as possible so that the others may group themselves around him, or rather round his wife, who cooks and milks for them all. Otherwise the brothers may scatter to the homes of their married sisters, of their mothers' brothers, or of some other kinsmen. Even after men are married and have homes of their own there are many occasions when they have to rely on the wives of brothers or of other neighbours and kinsmen for the milking of their cows. Nuer group themselves round a herd, and the rule prohibiting men from milking means that in grouping themselves around a herd they also group themselves around the milkmaid who serves the herd. This central position a wife has in Nuer economy, like the central position she has as a mother in the lineage, to which I have earlier referred, enhances her status in society. Here again also her position in this respect as in the other tends to break down narrow family exclusiveness and to draw closer to her husband his brothers and close paternal kin.

The family produces most of what it needs, and most of what it produces it consumes. Nevertheless, some tasks cannot be performed, and others are often not performed, by the ordinary family without assistance from kith and kin; and there is much sharing among neighbours. Most hunting, and much of the fishing, require more participants than the family can muster, and unless families take it in turn to herd, a single family would find it difficult or impossible, especially in dry-season camps, to look after its cattle, calves, sheep, and goats, as well as to attend to the children and the tasks of kraal and kitchen. Help in activities requiring co-operation, as well as in milking when that is required, is given by close neighbours who are also kinsmen. Also, there are other tasks which, though they might be accomplished by the family unaided, are often, but by no means always, performed by co-operative parties of neighbours: clearing gardens, making drainage trenches, dams, and seed-beds in swampy ground, weeding, harvesting, threshing, and building. The helpers are given beer or porridge or both. Thus Nuer say of building a byre: 'We Nuer cut the supports with beer, we cut the grass with beer, we build the walls with beer, and we erect the supports with porridge.' Although a family probably spends as much labour in helping other people as would, had it been expended in their own home and gardens, have enabled them to be self-sufficient in maintaining them, it is much more pleasantly spent when distributed in this way. Not only is a family relieved of the necessity of tackling particularly laborious jobs unaided, but when the work is done by mutual aid it becomes something of a game, losing its monotony in merry company and in the feelings of good-neighbourliness it engenders; for the beer and porridge are not payment for work done but hospitality provided for friends and kin, who accept the invitation to take part in the work because they are friends and kin. The owner of the homestead does not supervise the work, and each does as much or as little as he chooses. Apart from co-operative parties of this kind Nuer, especially the women, prefer to perform their like, but several, duties in company where this is convenient, as when women collect wild fruits or draw water, boys herd the goats and sheep, and men fish with spears in pools, lagoons, and the shallows of streams.

A kinsman is also expected to help another who is in need by giving him what he is in need of if he is in a position to do so. Nuer say that 'among kinsmen of every kind there is no purchase' and that 'with us Nuer, it is all giving and begging'. Also, Nuer eat so much in each other's byres and windscreens that, as far as the men are concerned, there may be said to be to some extent com-mensalism among the members of nearby homesteads and even between the members of a small village. Nuer keep open house and, in their summer camps especially, men visit one another so regularly to drink milk together that an older man does not care to drink milk alone but sends a small boy to invite an age-mate to share his gourd with him. Nuer readily lend milch cows to fami-lies with small children and make gifts of millet and fish to those in need. When animals are sacrificed the meat is generally the right of a family, or of a family and their close kin, but neighbours often receive meat if they ask for it persistently enough, for it is not thought mean to refuse. On some occasions a beast belongs to whoever can seize meat from it, but on such occasions men of the same household assist one another, and as those taking part in the scrimmage are all kith and kin a sense of fairness prevails. In general it may be said that no one in a Nuer village starves unless all are starving. The food supply of a community is ultimately at the disposal of all its members within whose corporate life each family has security to pursue its particular interests and to satisfy its most elementary needs.

II

Though I did not study in detail relations within the Nuer family, I could not have avoided reaching some general conclu-sions about them, and I set these down here in so far as they relate to the kinship system and the life of the wider society, the values of which, reflected in modes of address, are assimilated to those obtaining within the family.

Nuer have told me, though they do not like to speak of it, for it touches on death, that there is what we would call a latent hostility between husband and wife, and indeed between man and woman. They say that when a man has begotten several children by his wife he wants her to die, and may even pray for this to happen, for he does not want to die before her and another man to cohabit with her, rule in his home, use his cattle, and perhaps ill treat his children and rob them of their birthright. Men say also that women in their hearts wish for their husbands' deaths. Whatever may be the significance that should be attached to these statements and to stories in which similar sentiments are expressed, family life among the Nuer is remarkably harmonious on the surface. I attribute this, in part at any rate, to the unchallenged authority of the husband in the home. A woman must obey her husband, and Nuer say that when he swears at her she must not answer back, and that he has the right to chastise her if she neglects her children or domestic duties. They told me that should he kill her (I have never heard of a case of the kind), whatever trouble his action may otherwise bring on him, he will not have to pay compensation, for she belongs to her husband's people and he only destroys what is his own, losing thereby both wife and the cattle he paid for her. No doubt there are cases of cruelty, especially where captive Dinka women are concerned, and I have been told of such, but I must record that during a year spent in intimate contact with Nuer in villages and camps I did not once see a man strike his wife or hear a serious quarrel between spouses, and I believe therefore that these are rare happenings.

Women know their duties and unless they are by nature lazy and slovenly, or wish to goad their husbands into divorcing them, they avoid domestic shortcomings. The husband, for his part, does not interfere with his wife's organization of her duties. So long as she performs them she may do so in her own way. For instance, when there is meat, a man hands it to his wife to prepare and leaves it to her discretion to decide how much of it to keep for herself and her children and how much to serve to the menfolk in the byre. Moreover, it is difficult for a man to ill-treat his wife, even should he wish to do so, for his conduct cannot be kept secret and his kinsmen would certainly intervene on her behalf. I have been told that no reputation in Nuerland is more shameful than that of a wife-beater, a man who prefers *kur man*, fighting with women, to *kur wutni*, fighting with men. Also, a Nuer woman—a Dinka captive is not in so favourable a position—who readily accepts admonishment and correction for faults, would not submit to bullying but would return. to her parents and brothers, leaving her husband without cook, dairymaid, and nurse, and therefore unable to maintain his home; and he might find it difficult to persuade her to return. If she does return it will only be after lengthy discussions in her parents' home and, as he is likely to have said something unpleasant about them in altercations with his wife, he may have to pay them a cow in compensation. Even if her father and brothers support her husband, he cannot prevent her from running away again, and this time to some distant relative who is unconcerned alike whether the bridewealth is returned or what the husband's grievances and discomforts may be. Should he decide to divorce her and marry again, he has first to get his cattle back—it is always doubtful whether he will succeed in doing so—and he has then to face two or three years as a bachelor before his new wife comes to live with him. Therefore he will only take this step if his wife shows that she is determined to leave him, or if she is incorrigibly lazy, dirty, foul-mouthed, quarrelsome, or wanton, and occasionally if she is barren. Even if she has these defects he may, rather than go through the tedious process divorce entails, let her depart and bear him children by other men. A man will seldom divorce his wife for adultery unless she is constantly unfaithful.

With rare exceptions, I found Nuer women well content with their station and that their husbands and other men treated them with respect. In saying that their status in society is high I am judging not so much by the fact that the same number of cattle have to be paid for the homicide of a woman as of a man, and I believe more for a young woman in some parts of Nuerland, but by the part women take in the daily life of the community. They mix freely and with easy assurance with the men, and they do not hesitate to argue with them about matters in which they are interested as women. They have as intimate relations as the men with the cherished cattle, share with them the life of the kraal, and enter the byres when they wish to do so.

In a polygamous family the relations between husband and wife are complicated by the husband's relations with his other wives. *Nyak*, a co-wife, in its verbal form means both 'to be a co-wife' and,

ominously, 'to be jealous'. The first wife has no special status,
though the husband generally consults her more than the other
wives because he married her first and started his home and family
with her. On the contrary, Nuer insist on the equality of wives,
and they recognize that custom of the home is intended to elimin-
ate as far as possible friction between them. The wives generally
cook in turn for the husband and the byre, and each cooks as well
for herself, her daughters, and small sons; but it is also a convention that a wife shall frequently cook for the family of a co-wife
and that the children of one hut may eat in any other hut. I was
told that if there is any trouble between the huts this convention
is unlikely to be observed. Nuer have told me also that some
women, while they give food they have cooked to their co-wives,
remove part of it before doing so and hide it for their own children
to eat in secret; and there is even a word for this part. It is impressed
on boys that when they bring fish or meat to the home they should
not give it to their own mothers but to another of their father's
wives. A man would never address one of his mother's co-wives as
'ciek gwar', 'my father's wife', but either as 'ma', mother', or by
some honorific title; and she would reply 'gatda', 'my son', and not
'gat nyakda', 'son of my co-wife'. Indeed, there is the same kind of
assertion, in the face of reason and experience, that 'ciek gur',
'your father's wife', is 'mor', 'your mother', as is made when Nuer
say that 'gat gur', 'your father's son', is 'demor', 'your mother's
son'; and the two assertions are different sides to the same dogma,
to a further consideration of which I shall return. But though
children are told that their father's other wives should not be
treated differently from their mother, it seems to be acknowledged
by all that there is likely to be jealousy between co-wives, especially if the husband appears to favour one wife or her children,
and that it is a misfortune for children should their mother die
and they be left to the care of a co-wife. Nuer say that this is what
happened to gukur, the dove, and is the reason for its plaintive
note 'giek ciek gur', 'bad is your father's wife'.

Before considering briefly relations between parents and children it is, I think, important to recognize that a Nuer child is not
born into the family alone and then slowly extends his awareness
to members of the household and kin, but is born into a wider
circle than the family, in the sense that all those who share the
homestead of the father and adjacent homesteads take an interest

in the child from the time the mother leaves her hut after bearing him. The father's other wives, his brothers and their wives, and other kinsmen and affines of the father if they live near him, take

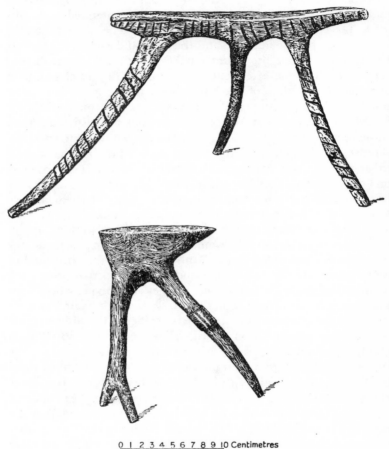

0 1 2 3 4 5 6 7 8 9 10 Centimetres

Wooden neck-rests or pillows

frequent notice of the child, nurse him, talk to him, and make him understand that they belong to him. If he is an eldest child and is brought up in his maternal grandparents' home, he will have the same close relations with corresponding persons there.

Nuer welcome children and hope when they marry that their

wives will be fertile. Abortion is said to be very rare and practised only by unmarried girls. Though the men of the kraal may hope that monorchids and babies born with defects and deformities will not survive, they do not kill them or let them die. The proper care and nurture of children is the concern of the whole family and household, and from the moment of birth care is taken to isolate the child from any contact which might be injurious to it. Even the father keeps away from the mother's hut for the first few days lest he inadvertently cause it some misfortune. The prohibition on coitus between parents till the child is weaned is seldom infringed, although it imposes long abstinence, for the child is suckled till he can digest solid food and can toddle about homestead and camp by himself. Artificial aids to weaning are rarely necessary, infants passing slowly from the breast to cow- and goat-milk, though sometimes they are sent to their maternal grandparents for some weeks to make the break. Children have first claim in the allocation of milk from the herd, and if there is a shortage it is the adults, and not they, who go without.

The care of small children falls naturally to the mother, and it is she who feeds and bathes them and attends to their other wants. But the father also takes an interest in his infant children, and one often sees a man nursing his child while the mother is engaged in the tasks of the home. Nuer fathers are proud of their children and give much time to them, petting and spoiling them, giving them titbits, playing with them, and teaching them to talk; and the children are often in the byres with the men. The affection of children for their fathers is very striking in Nuerland. I have never seen a man beat his child or lose his temper with him, however aggravating he might be. When a father speaks crossly to his child, as he does if, let us say, the child goes to the edge of a river or among the cattle, where he may be injured, it is evident that the child is not afraid of his loud words and obeys from affection rather than fear. In his first years a child is corrected by his mother and elder brothers and sisters, who may give him a few strokes with a grass switch if he is naughty.

Daughters grow up under the direction of their mothers. Mother and elder sisters give a girl training in household tasks and what moral advice and worldly wisdom they care to impart. The father takes little interest in the affairs of his daughters. His chief concern with them is to ensure that they are well married.

Boys come under their father's direction. He and the other men of the kraal see that they carry out their duties in the care of flocks and herds. Boys learn from their elder brothers and cousins how to fish, hunt, cultivate, dance, flirt, and engage in the other activities of men. A boy can see the stages of his life before him—initiation, courtship, marriage, and the starting of a family and home—and he realizes even in childhood that these stages are bound up with his father's herd, and that he and his brothers have a common interest with their father in the herd. It is very noticeable that when boys talk about the cattle it is in reference to marriage and when girls talk about them it is in reference to milk.

In my experience, it is only when a father is selfish or extravagant in his use of the herd that, even when his sons are men, any serious disagreement is likely to arise between them. Even then, young men submit to their father's indiscretions. If they may show their disapproval by going to stay with relatives for a time they say little, partly, no doubt, because they fear a father's anger and curse, but chiefly, I believe, because, in spite of faults, they love and respect their fathers. Though relations between a father and his son may be strained, the sorrow and anxiety of the son should his father fall sick are most apparent. Nuer say that should father and son fail altogether to agree the son may go to live permanently with his maternal uncle, but this would be a most serious offence in the eyes of Nuer, being *dakene mar*, the breaking of kinship. I have never known it happen.

Boys treat their mothers with affection, though they are offhanded with them and are sometimes rude to them. When they are approaching the threshold of manhood a feeling of male superiority seems to affect their attitude to their mothers. I was told that a youth would never interfere on his mother's behalf should his father be angry with her, though should the father wish to beat her the son would not reveal her hiding-place lest she should curse him. A mother's curse prevents a man from begetting male children. Fear of it was the reason given me for the care Nuer take of their mothers when they are very old, carrying them on their shoulders from village to camp and from camp to village, but, here again, I think that natural affection is a stronger motive.

My observations of the relations between parents and children do not permit me to develop the subject beyond such general impressions as I have given. I would like, however, to draw attention to the peculiar position in each elementary family of the eldest child.* The eldest child of either sex is known as *gat ma keagh* and the mother may address him (or her) as *keaghda*, my first-born. This child must never use the spoon of his father or mother, and I have sometimes been given to understand that this is one of the reasons for the bringing up of an eldest child by his maternal grandparents, it being felt better to keep him away from his parents' home till he is of an age to observe the prohibition. He must also avoid sleeping or sitting on his mother's sleeping-hide, for this may make her barren and may also injure the father, the child himself, and the cattle. I believe also that if the eldest child is a girl she may not use the horns of female animals for any purpose. When an eldest male child is initiated an extra incision is made, at any rate in some parts of Nuerland, on his forehead—seven instead of the usual six—and an ox must be sacrificed at the ceremony, whereas a goat or sheep may be considered sufficient for a younger son. Parents, especially the mother, and maternal uncles are said to fear the curse of an eldest child.

These customs relating to the eldest child are an indication of his special position in the family and kinship system. He is born in his mother's home and ought to be brought up there if his maternal grandmother is alive. If she is dead the child will probably be brought up by his parents till he is about six years of age, and then go to his maternal uncle till puberty. The eldest child is the keystone of the marriage. Till he is born the marriage is not regarded as complete. He is also the link through which the kin of the father and the kin of the mother are brought into relations of kinship with one another, for the child is the child of the mother's people as well as the child of the father's people. It is true that he belongs to his father's lineage, because he is the child of their cattle, but the sentimental claim of his mother's people to their daughter's child is recognized in their right to bring the child up in their home.

Indeed it must be acknowledged that in Nuer family life there is always a pull on the children in both directions: a pull of legal and religious norms and of the whole pattern of the politico-social

* The youngest child, the *pek*, also has a special position in the family, an indication of which in a male child is in some tribes the cutting of an extra line on his forehead at initiation, as in the case of an eldest male child. I am not cer tain, however, how socially significant is his position.

structure towards the father's kin and lineage, and a pull of personal affection towards the mother's people. Rights in the herd, duties of blood revenge, and status in the community hold a man to his father's kin, but with these go jealousy about cattle, resentment against authority, and personal rivalries. A man has no rights in his maternal uncle's herd, he has no obligation to assist his maternal uncle's people in their feuds, and he has no hereditary status in his maternal uncle's community. But the fact that he lacks these rights and duties and status means that he is not burdened with the disputes and tensions they engender. The paternal ties are stronger, if there is a touch of hardness in them. The maternal ties are weaker and for this reason are tenderer. In the Nuer family the tension is greatest in the case of the eldest child, especially an eldest son, for both families more strongly assert their rights in him than in the younger children, but it is inherent in the nature of the Nuer family and has also a more general social significance in the counter-attraction of the lineage on one side and the wider society on the other.

This pull in opposite directions, towards the father's kin and towards the mother's kin, is most evident in polygamous families, where the sons of each hut have different sets of kinsmen on the mother's side. I cannot say what is the frequency of polygamy in Nuer society, and it would in any case be difficult, in view of the variety of Nuer domestic unions, to decide on a criterion of polygamy; but though monogamous marriage is much commoner, polygamy is frequent enough to have set its stamp, through its association with wealth and social influence, on the lineage system. The polygamous family is for the Nuer the ideal form of family life and every man would like to attain to it. It has therefore importance out of all proportion to the actual number of such families. The values and the whole conception of the lineage system are reflected in it.

A Nuer lineage is often named after a woman, its ancestress, because lineages are generally thought of as dividing out from within a polygamous family. They cannot be differentiated by reference to the name of the father of the founders of the different lines of descent, but only by reference to the names of the founders themselves or of their mothers. Thus the typical lineage structure is conceived of as being present in the structure of the polygamous family and in the distribution of huts in the homestead it occupies.

This is why a lineage is generally called a *thok dwiel*, the entrance to the hut—not the byre—or a *thok mac*, the hearth of the fire at which women cook—not that around which men sit and sleep.

There is involved here a contradiction between the dogma of the unity of brothers, which the Nuer so often enunciate, and both the lineage system and the common experience of family life. It is a cardinal teaching that all brothers are equal and undivided, for they are all sons of the same father and therefore, through their identification with him, equivalent in the lineage. Maternal descent does not count within the lineage and therefore ought not to count within the family, for by the agnatic principle in Nuer social life the family derives from the father. Hence, Nuer say, if your uterine brother and your paternal half-brother quarrel you must not enter the dispute on your uterine brother's side, because by so doing you divide the family. You split, as it were, the father.

That the huts do not divide the byre is particularly emphasized by, and in, the rule, previously referred to in our discussion of bridewealth, that brothers must marry in order of seniority of birth, a division by age reinforced by the distinctions of the age-set system, irrespective of whether in each marriage the cattle of the bridewealth came into the family herd from the previous marriages of the particular brother's full or half-sisters. Also, all the brothers must marry before any one of them takes a second wife. Even after the father is dead, opinion enforces this rule. It is only when, as rarely happens, there are enough cattle for a further marriage from the herd before the younger brothers are old enough to take wives that an elder brother may marry a second wife before they are married. When a man dies his eldest son takes his place as head of the family: 'He changes himself into something like their father.' It is then his duty to see that his unmarried brothers are not unfairly treated. Should the family disperse and one of the brothers attempt to take for himself all 'the cattle of the mother' of his uterine sisters' marriages, and refuse to allow them to be used for the marriage of a half-brother who is the senior of the unmarried sons of the family, it might prove difficult to prevent his doing so; but were he to do so, he would cut himself off from his brothers and paternal kinsmen. They would not any more assist him in his troubles and quarrels. 'They may even let him be killed unaided and recoup themselves for his past meanness with the cattle they receive in compensation for his death.' This is the final and, to a Nuer, most frightful sanction.

Nuer feelings about this matter are reflected in their use of kinship terms. Although '*demar*' (or '*gatmar*') means 'my uterine brother' and '*gatgwar*' is the term for 'my father's son' (paternal half-brother), they almost invariably use the term for the uterine brother to refer to, or address, the half-brother and keep the term for 'father's son' to speak about or address paternal cousins. To address a father's son by the term for this relationship is regarded as very bad form because it makes a cleavage in the family. It would be even worse to call your full brother '*gatgwar*', 'my father's son'. The term would only be used for this person as an affectionate meiosis. In the same way, a man must not address his paternal half-sister by the term for this relationship ('*nyigwa*'), for '*nyagur e jen nyimor*', 'your father's daughter (paternal half-sister) is your mother's daughter (full sister)'. It is true, as will be seen in the next chapter, that there is a general tendency for Nuer to use kinship terms for persons who stand in a more distant relationship to those which they denote and that the terms '*demar*' ('*gatmar*') and '*nyimar*' are freely used for almost any person of a man's own generation, but Nuer particularly emphasize the need for this displacement in the case of half-brothers and half-sisters. Nuer have told me that they are so anxious not to distinguish between full and half-brothers that should a man go with his half-brother to visit his mother's sister's home, the young men of that home will make a point of greeting the half-brother first and of addressing him as '*gatmar*', 'son of my mother', before addressing their true mother's sister's son by this term (which correctly applies to him and not to his half-brother). I have earlier noted that the wife of one brother is spoken about as the wife of all the brothers and her children as the children of them all.

But although Nuer are constantly asserting the solidarity of the polygamous family, it is as evident to themselves as it is to the observer that things are often different. They recognize that whereas full brothers pool their resources, helping each other even to the point of forgoing their rights, paternal half-brothers insist on their rights and try to avoid their obligations, doing for each other only what self-interest demands of them. Nuer are not surprised at—they expect—coldness between half-brothers, and disagreements and disputes between them, and between paternal cousins, are endemic in Nuer society. Quarrels between half-brothers are a frequent theme in stories of the separation of lineages and the dispersal of paternal kin. They are the 'bulls' of whom I said in Chapter I that each goes his own way and seeks to gather round himself a separate cluster of kin and affines. Even when there are no disagreements half-brothers tend to drift apart after the death of their father, especially after they are married, and go to live with their different maternal and affinal kin.

However, sons ought to continue to live together on the death of their father, and it is hoped that they will do so. If they live together there is less chance of unfairness in the disposal of the cattle and of resultant disputes. A man may anticipate difficulties of the kind by directing before his death how his herd is to be divided among his sons. If he does not do this, it ought to remain undivided till all the sons are married. What is left of it may then be divided among them at a family council. There is more likelihood of this being done if all the sons live together, for then, even though the herd is divided among the huts, it is still very much a single herd in a common kraal. When one of the brothers wants to marry, the different huts will all 'loosen cattle' for his marriage, as they would have done had the father been alive. But if a widow takes her sons to her own kin or to the home of a lover in a distant part of the country, the half-brothers who remain in their father's home are less inclined to help them when they want to marry, and if they have no uterine sisters they may then find it difficult to do so. Nevertheless, a boy without uterine sisters is to some extent protected by the rules governing division of bridewealth, which ensure that he will receive at least some of the cattle of the marriages of his paternal half-sisters. He will also receive cattle on the marriages of other female relatives: the daughters of his father's brothers and sisters and the daughters of his mother's brothers and sisters. He may possibly also receive *wang-nen* cattle of his grandparents. Though he lives apart from them, his half-brothers will not seek to deprive him of his rights in bridewealth, even if they are not ready to help him by gifts from their own herds.

In discussing the shortcomings of half-brothers Nuer often further mention the obligation to marry a wife to the name of a man who dies without heirs. If he leaves behind an unmarried uterine brother, this brother will use the cattle brought into the home on the marriage of one of their sisters to take a wife in his name. If he had only half-brothers it is feared that they may try to 'blot out' the dead man's name and use the cattle to marry wives in their own names. To prevent this it is said that the dead man's mother's people may, if there was no close friendship between him and his half-brothers, arrange for his uterine sister to marry a wife to his name. Her husband then takes the cattle which would have gone to the dead man on the marriages of his sisters and makes the arrangements for his wife to marry a wife to his name with them, though he does not himself cohabit with this wife. Nuer say that in affairs of this kind a sister's son can be trusted better than a paternal half-brother. As I have mentioned in the last chapter, the disposal of widows may occasion rancour among paternal half-brothers.

The distinction between full and half-brothers runs right the way through the Nuer kinship system. Nuer say that *'gurlen kwi dwiel'*, 'your father's brother on the side of the hut' (his uterine brother), is a real father to you, but *'gurlen kwi luak'*, 'your father's brother on the side of the byre' (his paternal half-brother), is only a father in his talk. If your father is dead and you are still a boy he may take advantage of your youth to deprive you of your rights. Similarly, Nuer say that the *nar mande* (or *nar kwi dwiel*), the mother's uterine brother, is a real mother and father, but not the *nar gwande* (or *nar kwi luak*), the mother's paternal half-brother. I once asked a youth who was threatening to fight his maternal uncle over an insult he considered he had received from him, 'But surely he is your maternal uncle?' 'Yes,' he replied, 'but only a maternal uncle on the father's side.'

When we speak of uncles on the byre-side we speak of half-brothers of the parents who own their own herds and homesteads, maybe in different villages, districts, or even tribes. They have already become distinct points of growth on the lineage branch. There is no pretence here that they are undivided. This dogma does not go beyond the family: sons in relation to their father. As we have seen, within the family it is the assertion of an ideal in the face of recognized social actualities which only partly conform to it; for the difference between full and half-brothers, or between the huts, in a family is both marked and a matter of concern to Nuer. It is clearly connected with the lineage structure and with the importance of the maternal kin in social life, which is related

VIII. The leaping movement (*rau*) in a dance

to that structure, for both act to pull apart the children of different wives of the same husband.

I shall return to the distinction between full and half-brothers when discussing the Nuer kinship system. We will then see how categories of relationship fall into two broad classes: the 'bulls', the paternal kin and members of the lineage, and those traced in one way or another through women, the *gaatnyiet*, the children of girls. Half-brothers are 'bulls', but full brothers, who form the closest of all relationships except for that of twins,* are not only paternal kin but also maternal kin. A full brother 'is like your mother and your father'.

III

Complicated patterns of family relationships arise from the different forms of domestic union I described in the last chapter, and a rather lengthy discussion of them cannot be avoided.

Often there is opposition between the interests of the legal family and the interests of these other bio-domestic groups; that is to say, between the interests of the group united by marriage and descent and the interests of the procreative group united by common residence and life. When a child is a member of both groups it sometimes happens that the privileges he derives from membership of the one clash with his feelings towards the people of the other. The extent to which this opposition affects the lives of the persons concerned depends on conditions which vary in each case. It is impossible in advance to know how any particular person will be affected, and one can only guess how he will act when one knows the characters as well as the status of the people involved. But the normative principles that govern the behaviour of parents and children may be explained. In any particular case their actions will tend to follow the lines here laid down. Only the position of sons is considered. Daughters will not remain with either their genitor or the kinsmen of their pater, but will become members of their husbands' households. Control over their persons is therefore not disputed, and division of their bridewealth is so well defined by custom that it is a matter of minor importance where they are brought up.

* Twins have a peculiar social position, being treated as one person, and are the object of special observances which I have described in detail in the *Uganda Journal* (1936).

The simple legal family in which husband and wife are both legal and natural parents of the children has great cohesion and permanent lines of descent join father and sons. It has the advantage over the other domestic groups under discussion that the formal status of its members towards one another is generally in harmony with their sentiments. For example, the respect and affection of a son for a father are directed towards a legal father. Also, even when there is friction between son and father, there is no opposing group to which the son can attach himself without losing to some extent the privileges of his birthright. This is the sense of a remark made to me by a youth who was openly on bad terms with his father: 'If he (my father) had been my genitor only (and not my pater) I would long ago have left him and started a kraal of my own.' A youth is firmly bound to his family from motives of self-interest no less than from habit and sentiment of home. If he leaves them he will not go to live at the home of another man he calls 'father' but with his mother's kin or with affinal relations.

When a man marries a wife to the name of his father or brother or paternal uncle, the relations between the members of the group that ensues are the same as those between members of a simple legal family during the childhood and boyhood of the sons, as far as can be judged by behaviour and expression of sentiment, and it is only in legal alinement that the groups differ; but when the sons become men there is a significant difference between them. A son of a simple legal family has no property rights independent of his father. But when, for example, a man has married a wife in the name of his paternal uncle, the son he begets is his father's brother's son and belongs to a different family to that of the man who begat him. When the son grows up his legal personality is merged in that of his dead pater, whose status he assumes and whose property rights he inherits. If the pater left cattle the genitor ought to have held them in trust for his sons. Even if the pater, as is often the case, had no cattle when he died, he had potential rights in his family herd and in the bridewealth of sisters and kinswomen, and these rights his sons inherit. Consequently, if a son born in the union of ghost-marriage does not agree with the man who stands in the place of his pater, he is able more easily to take up an independent position than a son born of simple legal marriage. However, I know of no serious dispute between a ghost-son and his genitor where they are paternal kin, for the genitor stands in the place of the pater and has the same desire to see his sons, having probably no legal children of his own, happy and wealthy as a pater has. A ghost-son is generally content to see his genitor dispose of his cattle during his boyhood, knowing that when he is old enough to marry he will be provided for.

When a man marries a wife in the name of his maternal uncle a difficult situation may arise. Such a marriage usually takes place when the dead man has no close paternal kinsmen; and the sister's son often marries the wife with part of the uncle's herd and takes charge of the remainder of it. In childhood the relations between parents and children are the same as those in a ghost-family in which pater and genitor are paternal kinsmen, but when the sons grow up differences between them and their genitor are likely to be acute if the genitor has abused his trust. It is less an abuse for a paternal kinsman to use the dead man's cattle for his own purposes, since they both belong to the same agnatic and cattle-group, than for a sister's son to do the same, for the sister's son is not a member of the lineage of the pater and has no rights in their cattle. When the daughters he begets by his maternal uncle's wife are married he ought to keep the cattle of their bridewealth till the brothers of the girls are old enough to marry with them. Nevertheless, he may take advantage of their minority. Since the dead man's paternal kin are unlikely to be very close kin, they may do little beyond protesting, especially if, as is probable, the sister's son lives among them; but there is almost certain to be bad feeling in the family. The position of the sons is difficult, and the conflict between their regard for their genitor, whom they have always regarded as their father in every practical sense, and their resentment at the injustice done to them may only be solved by their going eventually to join the household of some paternal kinsman of their pater.

If he is to avoid trouble a man who cohabits with his brother's widow must likewise remember that her children, whether begotten by the dead man or by himself, are his wards and that he is trustee and not owner of his brother's herd. When the eldest son has been initiated into manhood he takes the place of his pater as head of the family. If his guardian is wise he will respect his nephew's independent status and will build him a byre next to his own and give him the cattle to which he is heir. Then difficulties between them need not arise, and his nephews will retain their respect and affection for him and will share their cattle with him. But Nuer are greedy where cattle are concerned, and the temptation to use a dead brother's herd and the bridewealth of his daughters to marry wives for himself during the minority of his sons is sometimes more than a man can resist. When his nephews grow up they find that he has no cattle left for them to marry with and they are resentful and want to know what has happened to their father's herd. A nephew in this position is unlikely to move away from the village in which he has been brought up because it is his own village where his paternal kinsmen live, but his relations with his uncle may become strained and he may harden in his insistence on his full legal rights in future instead of accepting a friendly give-and-take arrangement. If exasperated beyond endurance, he may go to live elsewhere, perhaps with his maternal kin. Here again conflicting loyalties may make a youth's position difficult, for as a son he feels he ought to respect and obey his father and as a nephew he feels he ought to insist on his rights. Trouble is most likely to arise when a boy falls under the guardianship of a brother of his dead pater and is not begotten by him.

The opposition between the legal family and the natural family is most evident when a son is born in widow-concubinage. In ghost-marriage and leviratic marriage the genitor is a legal substitute for the pater, but the genitor of a child born in widow-concubinage has no such status. When the brothers of the pater are alive and family feeling is strong they insist on his sons being initiated in his home and living with them afterwards. Nuer say that an orphan who has been initiated at his uncles' home and has rights in cattle there will not want to leave it. They are likely also to bring the dead man's daughters to live with them so that they can be married from their home. The genitor cannot deny them their right when they tell him that they want the children of their cattle. Thus it often happens that a boy is brought up in one social group but belongs legally to, and later joins, a different social group. The sentiments of childhood attach him to the home of his mother and genitor, and while he is small he does not think of any other place as his home. But when he reaches manhood the sense of paternal kinship so strong in Nuer, and desire for the cattle of his heritage, attract him to the village of his true paternal kinsmen.

If a dead man has brothers they are almost certain, especially if they are uterine brothers, to want their child to live among them. Where we find adult sons living with their natural fathers in Nuerland it generally means that they have no close paternal kin. Or it may mean that the genitor is rich in cattle while the paternal kin, though close kin, are poor. A youth with close kin who possess herds does not care to live in the home of his genitor after his initiation, for he is always regarded there as to some extent an outsider, whereas in the home of his pater he is there by right of birth: 'He will visit his mother and the man who begat him now and again, sometimes for a month or two, but his home is the home of his dead father.'

A youth's allegiance also to some extent depends on the circumstances of the widow-concubinage in which he was born. If his natural father lived apart from his mother and merely visited her from time to time he counts for little, but if he shared her home he is of greater importance and his children will retain their affection for him and pay him frequent visits should he be later separated from them. Knowing how powerful an influence feelings of kinship and cattle interests will have on his sons when they grow up, he tries to win their love when they are small so that it may endure all the changes of life. 'When a man has a son by a widow-concubine he wishes the child to be with him the whole time so that when the child grows up he will know him and not desert him but remain in his home.' If a lover wins the affection of his sons in this way he may be able to keep them with him, especially if he and the paternal kinsmen of the sons occupy the same village, for sons generally wish to live after initiation with their paternal kin. Should he and the widow live elsewhere the sons are likely to part from them. This is a great stumbling-block to Nuer. 'You think how when they were little you carried them in your arms and played with them and fed them with titbits, and now they have gone to live with a man who did not bring them up, because it was with his cattle that their mother was married.' The sons are almost certain to depart sooner or later and for one reason or another. When their genitor has a legal family of his own they may feel neglected. If he has no legal family of his own it is because he has no cattle. Also he loses all hope of keeping the children if he loses the mother, for they are attached to him through her; and widow-concubines often change their lovers. Nuer say also that 'when a widow-concubine has finished bearing children she has no more use for her lover'. They say further that the lover of a widow has no chance of keeping sons begotten by her dead husband, however good a foster-father he may have been to them. 'A boy who knew his father does not forget him.'

But though children leave their natural father, the tie between him and them is never entirely severed. Even when a genitor has had little to do with his children a mystical tie unites them to him, so that Nuer say that if he is ill-disposed towards them they may suffer injury. Also, a natural son recognizes all the near kin of his genitor as his own kin and they acknowledge him to be their kinsman. When a man has been on intimate terms with his natural children the tie is much stronger. In his district they are called after him. A man may sacrifice a bull in honour of his genitor as well as in honour of his pater, and if his genitor did not beget legal children he may marry a wife to his name. *Liem*, the begging of a gift, is said by Nuer to be the most typical expression of the relationship between a man and his natural father. A father is not likely to refuse his natural son's appeal for help, and if he can, he will assist him to marry. He knows that his generosity will be rewarded by frequent visits.

Something has been said about the relation between sons and fathers in simple legal marriage, ghost-marriage, leviratic marriage, and widow-concubinage. It remains to say a few words about that between a son of an unmarried concubine and his pater. His position is very different from that of the son of a widow-concubine. 'A son of an unmarried concubine is your own son.' So long as you are kind and generous to the boy he will not desert you, for you are both his genitor and his pater and if he leaves you he has no other father to whom he can go. If the mother leaves her lover and goes to live with another man, the father of their children will put no obstacles in the way of their visiting her when they choose. He is confident that a son, even though he is a child, will return to him, 'because he is old enough to know his father, for when his father kills an animal he will keep meat for him to eat, and when food is served in the byre he will call his little son to eat with him'. An unmarried concubine who goes to live with another man will probably remain with this man if she bears him children, but she is likely to return to her first lover to be with her children by him if she bears no children to her second lover. Nevertheless, the son of an unmarried concubine is not so strongly bound to his father as a *gat ghok pany*, a true child of cattle, that is to say, a child born of a legal marriage. If a boy born of an unmarried concubine is dissatisfied with his lot in his father's home, or if his father dies, he may go to live with his mother's people.

The personal relations engendered by all these diverse forms of family life present a picture of changing configurations which are most confusing. The flux, movements and comings and goings, we noted in our survey of local communities is here again evident in domestic life; and here again beneath the apparent confusion in personal relations we perceive how in the lineage system the dynamic process is slowed down and stabilized into structure. Individuals and families seem to float about, as it were, and lead an independent existence, but they are anchored always to some lineage by the agnatic principle, which decrees not only that every man must have a pater but that through a pater he must be attached to a lineage. We noted in the first chapter how, if persons become permanently detached from their own lineage, as captured Dinka do, they may attach themselves through female links, regarding them as paternal links, to another lineage, take root in its stem, and become part of its growth.

Here again we observe that the wider groups of paternal kin and lineage gain at the expense of the family, especially when it is a natural and not a legal family. The position of the father in these unions other than that of simple legal marriage is to a greater or lesser degree undermined by attachment of greater legal significance to the pater, who represents the principle of the lineage. Another important consequence, which will be better appreciated later, is the effect of these unions on kinship relations. We have noted that there is a balance in the kinship system between the paternal kin and the maternal kin and that this balance is felt in the pull on children, especially in polygamous households, in both directions. It is particularly evident also in the case of the unions I have described because the splitting of the roles of the father, and in the case of children of unmarried concubines the attachment of children of the same mother to different legal fathers, increases the bias towards the mother's side.

CHAPTER V

KINSHIP

I

A MAN's kin are those persons with whom he is genealogically connected through his father and mother. This does not mean that kin relationships are merely an extension of relationships within the family. The kinship system exists in its own right, and a child who is born into a family is born at the same time into a kinship system. Nor does it mean that kin relationships are of the same order as family relationships. They are not—certainly to a Nuer. To him, his father and mother and brothers and sisters are not *mar*, kin, and he does not speak of them as such. They are members of his *gol*, his family, the intimate circle which he sees as something quite distinct from kin, just as we do when we say that someone is a relative and not a member of the family or that another is almost one of the family.

I have said earlier that anyone to whom a man can trace relationship of any kind, or to whom he merely knows that he stands in a certain category of relationship without knowing its degree, is in the wide sense of the Nuer term *mar*, kin, to him. I have shown that this means in fact that everybody in his village and those with whom he has dealings outside it are either true kin or are in one way or another treated as such.

Kinship categories are limited in number and they have a definite arrangement to any person. It is not merely that the anthropologist perceives that they have a pattern. The Nuer himself perceives it and can describe it without reference to any particular person, or as an abstract system. Also, when the pattern is enunciated in behaviour and there is no one to fill one of the roles, it is recognized that the actual configuration does not correspond to the ideal configuration, and that it should be made to conform to it by substitution, if this is possible.

In the arrangement of categories, and in the attention paid to them, there is a recognized balance between the kin on the father's side and the kin on the mother's side, and this balance is emphasized on certain formal occasions, above all in the notation of bridewealth rights when a marriage is being discussed. When a girl is married the bridewealth is, as we have seen, distributed among the following categories of kin: *gwanlen*, father's brother, *wac*, father's sister, *nar*, mother's brother, *manlen*, mother's sister, *gwandong*, father's father and mother's father, and *mandong*, father's mother and mother's mother. When a man is killed and cattle are paid in compensation, the cattle which are not reserved for marrying a wife to the name of the dead man are divided among the kin on the same principle as obtains for division of bridewealth. When an elephant is killed its tusks, or the cattle obtained for them by exchange, are divided among persons standing in the same set of relationships to the slayers of it. I believe also that when in the old days large numbers of cattle were taken on raids on the Dinka they were similarly divided among the kin of their captor. Though shares in these situations are the *cuong*, right, of the categories of kin I have mentioned, one cannot in any particular instance know for certain to which person a share will go because there may be more than one person standing in a certain category of relationship to a bride, a slain man, a killer of an elephant, or a raider of cattle; or the person to whom it would have gone had he been alive is dead and his right is inherited by his sons. But the right of the relationship is an absolute right. Bridewealth rights, in particular, are the most rigidly formulated of all the privileges of kinship. A man may neglect, elude, or defy the more fluid customary duties to kin without severing the bonds of kinship or even without seriously weakening them, but refusal to give a man the bridewealth cattle to which he is entitled is a total breach of kinship. It is not merely that those who refuse a man his right in this matter would be refused their rights by him when his daughters were married. The refusal cuts a man off from his kin altogether.

These categories of kin are again clearly defined by their representation in the distribution of sacrificial meat at weddings and other important feasts among the family and kin. There are variations in the allocations in different parts of Nuerland, but the same kin are everywhere represented in the distribution. The ideal distribution is usually cited in pairs of relationships in the same manner as the ideal distribution of bridewealth, bloodwealth, and elephant tusks is described: 'The right hindleg is the right of the father's brother and the left hindleg is the right of the mother's brother; the right foreleg is the right of the father's sister and the left foreleg is the right of the mother's sister'; and so forth. In the case of the uncles the allocations are further distinguished by defining whether the recipients are full or paternal half-brothers of father and mother. Some of the kinsmen who have a right to meat may be dead or absent, and it then goes to an heir or to someone standing in the same kinship category as the missing person. On the other hand, there may be several persons of the same category present, in which case the joint is divided among them. The joints may be described by reference to the relationships which have rights in them. On these occasions some of the meat given to a kinsman as his right may be eaten by him and his age-mates together, since a man's age-mates may have secondary rights in it. Representatives of collateral lineages, the *jibuthni*, also have rights in sacrificial meat. When beer is provided on certain ceremonial occasions it is distributed in the same manner as sacrificial meat among the kin on the father's side and the kin on the mother's side, and here again the recipients may share their pots with their age-mates.

Another situation in which the categories of kinship are ceremonially defined is the bringing of gifts at certain sacrifices, particularly those performed when a person has been killed by lightning, at mortuary ceremonies, when a man honours his dead father, and after the birth of twins. I have recorded some of these ceremonies elsewhere.* In describing what happens at a sacrifice in honour of a dead father a Nuer said: 'All your kinsmen are summoned on the day of sacrifice—the sons of your mother's sisters and the sons of your father's sisters, the sons of your mother's brothers and the sons of your father's brothers. Each brings beer to the sacrifice.' This way of speaking of the ceremonial functions of kin is almost a descriptive formula for the several rites I have just mentioned.

Apart from such formal definitions, Nuer speak of their close kinsfolk as their real (*pany*) kin as distinct from more distant kin. 'They are your real kinsfolk, they are the people who help you.' In spite of all disputes and shortcomings, a man's kin assist him in trouble. They help him in the more laborious tasks of his home.

* 'Customs Relating to Twins among the Nilotic Nuer', *Uganda Journal*, 1936; 'The Nuer *Col Wic*', *Man*, 1949; and 'Burial and Mortuary Rites of the Nuer', *African Affairs*, 1949.

They give him support by their presence at his rites. They nurse him when he is sick. They give him food when he or his children are hungry. They assist him to marry, often beyond their obligations, when he is poor, and in certain circumstances others besides those normally asked to contribute cattle will do so: for example, a man's sister's son or a widow-concubine with whom he is living. His kin rush to a man's assistance when he is in danger, the strength of kinship ties being very noticeable when quarrels break out, as they so frequently do in Nuerland, at dances. A man in difficulties then shouts for his kin and they rush to aid him without consideration of how the quarrel may have come about or who might be responsible for it, for he is a father's brother's son, a sister's son, a father's sister's son, or whatever it may be. Consequently those who attack a man must be ready to reckon with his kin also, and a man who cuts himself off from his kin faces disaster. If kinsmen find themselves facing one another in intercommunity fights they move to different positions in the lines to avoid having to fight each other.

It is true that it is particularly the duty of his paternal kin to help a man. It is their duty to avenge him if he is killed. They must hold a mortuary ceremony for his ghost when he dies. They must marry a wife to his name if he dies without male heirs. But if he has no close paternal kin, the kin among whom he has lived may perform these duties towards him. To break kinship (*dakene mar*) with the paternal kin is the worst of misfortunes. The man who does this can no longer claim rights in bridewealth or bloodwealth or sacrificial animals. If he is attacked his kinsmen look the other way, and he knows that if he is killed they will not avenge him. But to deny kinship with any close kin, maternal as well as paternal, is a misfortune. A man who wrongs a kinsman is shamed and he may incur also a curse and ghostly vengeance.

With his kin a man feels at ease. He does not, as we would say, have to keep up appearances with them. This is shown in one way by the manner in which kin swear (*kwith*) at one another. This is particularly the privilege of kin, who hurl the most abusive and obscene expressions at one another. Such behaviour is avoided in the family, though a man might swear mildly at his sister or even at one of his father's wives in anger, and it would almost certainly lead to a fight if an unrelated man were so insulted. Among kin, however, no offence is taken at abuse so long as it is an elder who abuses a younger, as an uncle a nephew, or the two are of the same generation, as between cousins.

The sentiment of *mar*, of communion with his kin, gives a Nuer the comfort of security, the feeling of being in a known and friendly world. I would again stress that *mar* is cognatic kinship, a set of relationships to any person through either father or mother and, among the Nuer, embracing also close affines, and further that in this general interpersonal sense one does not evaluate between the relationships. The maternal uncle is just as much kin as the paternal uncle, and the mother's sister's son as the father's sister's son. They are all people one helps when they need help and who help oneself when one needs aid. '*Jimarida*', 'my kin', are the people who are near me, irrespective of their precise category of relationship, the people on whom I can rely. It is interesting to note that *mar*, like the Old English 'sib', may also have the sense of 'peace'—'*te mar kamdien*', 'they are at peace'—and that it appears also to be the same word as that used for 'my mother'. In a sense all kinship is through the mother, even kinship with the father and hence with the paternal kin.

I have been speaking of the nuclear kin, but, as was noted in Chapter I, there is no limit to the number of relationships a man can in one way or another establish in Nuerland. The kinship system is like a circular elastic band which can be stretched on an ever-widening circumference as a child grows up and increases the number of his social contacts and enlarges the area of their distribution. By this wide recognition of kin a man thus brings in some degree his whole personal society, all those with whom he has dealings, into the circle of relationships in which attitudes and behaviour are shaped by sentiments of kinship.

I shall say more later about kinship in this wider sense and restrict my present remarks to the nuclear kin, which ordinarily can be regarded as the paternal and maternal uncles and aunts and their children and the children of brothers and sisters. A specific kinship term can be used to describe persons in each of these categories, and the relationships they embrace are the proto-types of all kinship ties of the wider kind.

II

These categories of relationship fall into two broad types. The first comprises the agnates, the kin of the byre-side, the 'bulls', as

Nuer would say, who are also referred to collectively and in a general way of speaking as the *gaatgwanlene*, the children of paternal uncles. We have noted how these are divided off as the kin *kwi gwan*, on the father's side (of the family), in division of bridewealth, and also how among themselves they are more or less exempted from the prohibition which defines as incest congress with the wives of kinsmen because their wives are all wives of the lineage. We have further noted that consciousness of being members of a social group with common ancestors and symbols and corporate rights in territory and, within the limited range of nuclear kin, common interests in cattle and wives and common residence pull the children of their wives to the father's side. The second broad type comprises the cognates who are not agnates, the kin on the hut-side, whom Nuer describe collectively and in a general sense as *gaatnyiet*, the children of girls or daughters—that is to say, all kin to whom a man is related through women. Either they are children of daughters of his lineage or he is the son of a daughter of their lineage. Within the restricted range of reference of bridewealth distribution these are the kin *kwi man*, on the mother's side (of the family). They are the kinsmen with whose wives it is incestuous to have congress. We have earlier noted how important this concept is in the network of kinship ties of any Nuer community, with regard both to interpersonal relations and also to the establishing of links with its dominant lineage. I shall have occasion later to emphasize further its significance in this respect in considering the kinship system in relation to society as a whole. The relationships in which these two types are, as it were, summed up and contrasted for a Nuer are that of the *gwanlen*, the paternal uncle, and that of the *nar*, the maternal uncle.

The *gwanlen*, particularly the father's paternal half-brother, is portrayed by Nuer as the wicked uncle and is contrasted with the good uncle, the *nar*, particularly the mother's uterine brother. Both youths and maidens have often told me that they are more at one with their mothers' brothers than with their fathers' brothers and with their mothers' sisters than with their fathers' sisters. 'Wa! Your *nar* is far better (than your *gwanlen*)', said a Nuer to me once, expressing with force this common partiality. When I asked him why the maternal uncle was better he gave no further answer than the usual reply to this question: 'Because he is the brother of your mother'. However, I pressed him for a fuller explanation, and he told me, as I have often heard from other Nuer, that you can rely on your maternal uncle for assistance. Even if your mother is dead he will gladly give you cattle to marry with, because you are the son of his sister and an orphan, whereas your paternal uncle, especially your father's half-brother, helps you reluctantly. If your paternal uncle is angry with you he may split your head open with his club, but however angry with you your maternal uncle may be, he would never strike you, for you are his sister's son.

I have been told time and again that Nuer youths whose fathers have died prefer to live with their maternal uncles, if they are full brothers to their mothers, than with their paternal uncles, though the father's full brother is regarded as a less formidable person than the father's paternal half-brother. The stereotyped portrait of a father's brother in the role of a step-father is of a selfish and mean man. Nuer say that if your father has died while you are still a child and his brother has taken your mother in leviratic union he will be kind to you for your mother's sake while you are a child, but when you grow up he will try to bully you and will be stingy with you. He will favour his own children and neglect you. Even if you are older than his own sons he may try to obtain wives for them first. What is worse, he may try to use your father's cattle and the cattle of your sisters' marriages for this purpose, or to marry another wife for himself, while you are still little and unable to protect your own. Your mother may be weak and consent to this wrong. His wives may give food to their sons who are still small boys while you, a man, have to wait for your portion; and when those boys are grown into men their mothers may hide food for them so that when you have shared the common bowl with them and rise from it still hungry they can eat again in secret and be filled.

A paternal uncle's obligation to assist his nephew to marry is another cause of bad feeling between them. We have noted that payment of bridewealth to kin is a legal obligation which involves the very principle of kinship and may in no way be avoided. The legal title to bridewealth on a girl's marriage implies a moral obligation to contribute cattle, though fewer than those received, to help her brother to marry, but it is an obligation which depends for its strength on personal relations and on ability to assist. It may not be carried out, and if it is not carried out the uncle does not thereby forfeit his title to bridewealth on the marriages of other sisters. Nevertheless, public opinion would censure a paternal uncle, or his son should he be dead, were he to refuse assistance, especially if, as is normally the case, they are living in the same or nearby homesteads. Paternal uncles are expected to help each of their nephews to marry in turn and to make a more generous contribution—perhaps two or three beasts at each marriage—than that looked for from the maternal uncle, for their nephews are their sons and are marrying wives to their lineage. The bulk of the bridewealth is provided by the family, but as the cattle of married brothers, though owned by them separately, are often herded together and tethered in the same kraal, the contributions by the father and his brothers may come from a single herd. Indeed, in a sense it is not easy to make a rigid distinction between what the father gives and what the uncles give towards the expenses of a marriage. The obligation on uncles is weightiest when they are full brothers of the father, live with or near him, and are on friendly terms with him. A half-brother of the father, especially if they live in different villages or districts, may feel that he has done all that should be required of him if he gives a beast on the marriage of one of his nephews. The younger brothers of the bridegroom must look for help to their other paternal half-uncles when it is their turn to marry.

The rivalry and conflict between paternal kin of which I have spoken comes out most clearly in relations between *gaatgwanlen*, male ortho-cousins, the sons of brothers, particularly of paternal half-brothers. Enmity between half-brothers is as far as possible suppressed, or at least not given public expression, on account of the father. If brothers disagree they separate, but they try to avoid scandal. Difference of generations inhibits either familiarity or declared hostility between a man and his paternal uncles, but the sons of these uncles are of his own generation and he can be as intimate or quarrelsome with them as he pleases. He is bound to them by ties of loyalty which do not derive from, or depend on, either mutual affection or common affection for a third person, as is the case with half-brothers who share the same father, and which generally necessitate close contact in situations likely some-times to engender conflict. It is perhaps this contradiction between social bonds and personal feelings which gives rise to the joking or teasing relationship between ortho-cousins.

I will not discuss here the use of obscene language in general among the Nuer but only the custom called *leng*, conventionalized exchange of obscenities, which is regarded as being pre-eminently a form of behaviour between paternal cousins of the same sex and generation, generally between males, whether they be first cousins or farther removed. It would be most improper for a man to exchange obscenities in this way with other kinsmen. A man says to a paternal cousin '*ban leng*', 'let us have a slanging-game'. Then they abuse each other in turn, prefacing each epithet with the exclamation *awai yah!* The exchange often develops into a contest to see which of the two can continue the longest without repeating himself. As Nuer are practised and have a fertile imagination in such matters, the duel may be kept up for several minutes before one of the men cannot think of an obscenity he has not already used and thus loses the duel, which is closed by shouts of laughter on both sides. The obscenities, which are the most extravagant I have ever heard, cover, with many elaborations, every possible kind of sexual act, the sodomy motif being the most prominent, and refer to the partners to the duel themselves and their fathers, mothers, sisters, paternal and maternal aunts and uncles, grand-parents, and sweethearts, though only terms of relationship and not proper names are used. The partners also call one another Dinka, witches, spongers, bastards, gluttons, and so forth. No offence is taken at the foulest sexual references to relatives, though I was told that paternal first cousins ought to avoid mentioning the father and the paternal aunt—'you do not do this because of your father'—and to restrict their observations to the mother and persons on her side of the family. Paternal cousins farther removed appear to feel no embarrassment in mentioning the father and his sister. However, paternal cousins avoid such exchanges in the presence of unrelated persons of the opposite sex.

The *wac*, father's sister, is not so prominent in the picture of family portraits as the father's brother because she is generally a member of a different local community, but Nuer say that she is like the father's brother: 'Your *wac* is your *gwanlen* also.' She may treat you badly when you are little, and even if she is kind she does not love you: 'The ones she loves are her grandchildren and the children of her sisters.' A Nuer told me that 'she thinks of you merely as "*gatdemar*" ("son of my brother")', by which he meant that she does not think of you as '*gatda*' ('my son'). She may talk friendly with you, but really she cares nothing for you and always favours her own children at your expense should you be living at her home. 'Your father's sister blesses you with her mouth, meaning nothing, but she cares nothing for you in her heart.' Nuer contrast her, especially the father's paternal half-sister, with the mother's sister, as they contrast the father's brother with the mother's brother. When you visit her she lets you remain hungry till evening instead of preparing a meal for you at once as a mother's sister would do. They also say that it is very likely she was resentful of your mother and takes it out of you. Nevertheless, a paternal aunt may be asked to assist her nephew to marry and with the consent of her husband, or son, she may contribute a heifer, though she is only likely to do so once. If there are several aunts and several nephews, one of the aunts will be asked for assistance on the marriage of one nephew and another aunt on the marriage of another nephew. Moreover, though the father's sister belongs to the 'bulls', her children are 'children of daughters' and the relationship of father's sister's son has the kindlier associations of this type of kinship.

It is only fair to say that the account given above is a gross distortion of the usual relations of a man with his paternal uncles and aunts, and indeed Nuer readily accept that they may be harmonious. They admit that many an orphan finds a true father in his father's brother and a true mother in his father's sister. They say that much depends on the character of the person concerned, the temper of relations between uncle or aunt and father and mother, and above all whether father and uncle have lived together, which often enough means whether they were full brothers, for then the uncle is one of those who has brought his brother's son up from childhood and regards him as much a son as a nephew.

I would remark here that, as was noted in our review of Nuer ideas about incest, though all paternal uncles and aunts are agnates, those who are uterine brothers and sisters of the father, while not, of course, in the Nuer sense of the word *gaatnyiet*, seem to partake in a kind of way of the quality of kinship through women just as, in a higher degree, the uterine brother does, for their kinship with the father is both on the byre-side and on the hut-side. They share with the father not only his paternal kin but his maternal kin also.

Nevertheless, distortion though it may be, it is a distortion which by over-emphasizing certain features of relationship on the paternal side brings out one of their essential characteristics, the personal rivalries generated by corporate life and common interests. It is understandable that those who live together have many opportunities for quarrelling and that their common interests, especially in regard to cattle in which they all have rights, provide occasion for it. A Nuer is bound to his paternal kin from whom he derives aid, security, and status, but in return for these benefits he has many obligations and commitments. Their often indefinite character may be both evidence of, and a reason for, their force, but it also gives ample scope for disagreement. Duties and rights easily conflict. Moreover, the privileges of agnatic kinship cannot be divorced from authority, discipline, and a strong sense of moral obligation, all of which are irksome to Nuer. They do not deny them, but they kick against them when their personal interests run counter to them. We noted in the last chapter that Nuer realize that the paternal half-brother relationship is one in the nature of which there are cleavage and opposition. In the nephew-paternal uncle and the ortho-cousin relationships the opposition is perhaps less tense because the persons belong to different families and households and their interests are more divergent, and because less effort has to be made to repress antagonisms. In their interrelations we have in embryo and between persons the same complementary tendencies towards fission and fusion that we find between opposed segments in the lineage system which derives from these paternal relationships as branches derive from twigs on a tree. We shall later see how the relation of the agnatic type of kinship to the type of relationship through women, and the relation of the lineage system to the whole society, are of the same pattern. First we must consider the categories of kinship on the mother's side of the family.

Nuer say of the maternal uncle that he is both father and mother, but most frequently that 'he is your mother'. He is a man's great supporter when he is in trouble. If a youth has committed adultery or involved himself in some other trouble, and his father's people refuse to aid him, he goes to his maternal uncle for help. He will help his sister's son for his mother's sake. Nuer say also that 'your maternal uncle will give you a cow and its calf to start a herd, and more cattle when you marry'. Indeed, he is expected at any time to give you a goat or a spear, or even a cow if he can afford it, when you are in need of these things, though you ought some day to make return to him. The relationship between sister's son and mother's brother is one of tenderness. Nuer have often told me how indulgent a mother's brother is with the little children of his sisters. They say, for example, that if a boy living at his maternal uncle's home feels out of sorts and does not want to spread out the cattle-dung to dry in the sun or to perform some other domestic task of boyhood, and the sons of the home think he is shirking work and abuse him, their father will admonish them to leave his sister's child in peace. If this happened at the home of a paternal uncle he would support his own sons and upbraid his nephew for laziness and even beat him. If a man's father is dead and his father's brothers have few cattle or are unfriendly towards him, he may go to live with his maternal uncle, and the uncle's wife will cook for him. He may even marry from the uncle's herd. Also, a youth during his father's lifetime often visits his mother's kinsmen and stays with them for weeks together. A Nuer lad has always a second home if his maternal uncle is a full brother to his mother. A mother's half-brother is regarded as a more distant person.

A man particularly looks for assistance from his mother's brothers when he wants to marry. If a mother's full brother likes his sister's eldest son he may give him two or three cows to help him get a wife, and he may make further contributions on the marriages of the younger sons. However, as in the case of the paternal half-uncle, a maternal half-uncle considers that he has done his duty if he assists one son of his sister's family to marry. He expects his next nephew to marry to approach his brothers for help. Even a maternal full uncle is not obliged to contribute to his nephew's bridewealth. If he refuses aid he cannot be deprived of cattle on the marriages of the young man's sisters. Any assistance he may give is regarded as an act of friendship and not as a return for the cattle he receives. The only cattle the mother's people are obliged to pay to her sons are a male and a female calf, which in eastern Nuerland are known as the *ghok jookni*, the cattle of the ghosts. This claim becomes due when the mother has reached the menopause.

The mother's brother-sister's son relationship is marked by a number of special observances. A youth at his initiation may ask his maternal uncle—generally it would be the mother's uterine brother—for a bull-calf with the markings of the new ox-name he has taken. Though he cannot demand it as a right, he may curse his uncle's herd so that the male calves die if he is refused his request. It seems that the customary way of making this request is for the nephew to make an incision on the ear of the calf he desires. A man may not bury his maternal uncle, and I believe that a mother's brother should not bury his sister's son. Were a man to bury his maternal uncle he would die of *keth nara*, a disease which is said to cause white patches on the skin. The same disease may attack a man who hears that his maternal uncle has been wounded or cut himself severely and does not visit him and place some of the blood on his foot. Should the nephew not hear of the uncle's wound and contract the disease, he visits him and gets him to rub soot from the bottom of a pot on the affected surfaces. A man and his maternal uncle may not tether their cattle together in the same kraal, though the cattle may graze together. If one of the uncle's beasts dies the nephew may not skin it, for were he to do so he would destroy the uncle's herd and people would say that 'he had spilt the cattle of his uncle to the ground'. An uncle may not give his sister's son a spear-shaft, for the gift might cause him serious injury. A man and his sister's son must not use the same sleeping-hide or sleep in the same hut. These rules, especially those which forbid a man tethering his cattle in his uncle's kraal, skinning his uncle's beasts, and sleeping in the same hut as his uncle, seem almost designed to keep the two apart, to prevent a youth identifying himself with his maternal kin instead of with his paternal kin.

The maternal uncle is the kinsman who most often blesses a lad in the Nuer way of blessing, by spitting on the head. Grandparents may sometimes do this, but other relatives rarely. If a man comes frequently to visit his sister and partakes of her hospitality and does not occasionally spit on her child's head, the child may get the disease I have mentioned above. It is also said that when a maternal uncle rises during the day from a nap in the ashes of the hearth and his sister's son rubs the ashes off his back he must then spit on the lad's head. But if the blessing of a maternal uncle is desired, his curse is believed to be among the worst, if not the worst, a Nuer can receive, for, unlike the father, a maternal uncle may curse a youth's cattle, as well as his crops and fishing and hunting, if he is disobedient or refuses a request or in some other way offends him. The curse may also prevent the nephew from begetting male children. Nuer therefore, however angry they may be, avoid swearing at their maternal uncles: 'Above all you must not swear at your maternal uncle. You might even think of swearing at your father but never, never, at your maternal uncle.'

It is the privilege of a maternal uncle's wife to swear abusively at her husband's sister's son. She does this teasingly and not in anger. He will not answer her back unless he is of about her age. A mother's brother's wife is often addressed by the anomalous term 'mandong', 'grandmother', though 'ma', 'mother', may also be used. When so addressed she answers her husband's sister's son as 'gatnyimar', 'son of my sister', or 'gatnyieti', 'son of daughters', 'on account of her husband whose sister bore him', and not as 'grandson'. Nuer have given me two reasons for this usage. I was told that 'after the mother of your mother has died she (your maternal uncle's wife) turns herself into something like your grandmother'. This corresponds to a man calling his wife's elder sister 'mother' when his mother-in-law is dead and respecting her as a mother-in-law. I was also told that 'you call her (your maternal uncle's wife) mandong (grandmother) because if he (your maternal uncle) dies you may take his wife'. Though in my experience this seldom happens, the second explanation is consistent with another anomalous usage, the description by a woman of her husband's sister as 'mancoada', which means literally 'mother of my husband', and of the son and daughter of her husband's sister as 'gatmancoada' and 'nyamancoada', 'my husband's mother's son' and 'my husband's mother's daughter'. In spite of these explanations it may be suggested that these peculiarities of behaviour and language relating to the maternal uncle's wife may be most appropriately interpreted in terms of the position of the maternal uncle in the kinship system.

The many observances relating to the mother's brother-sister's son relationship are indicative of this position, a further indication perhaps being the fact that, as will be seen in the following section, he alone among kinsfolk is not usually addressed by terms proper to the family. He is not, of course, strictly speaking a gatnyiet to his sister's son, but the relationship is one of this kind because his sister's children are gaatnyiet to him and his sons. Also in a general sense, in contrast to the 'bulls', the maternal uncle is a relative through a female, the mother. Indeed, he is spoken about by Nuer as a kind of male mother himself. The significance of his position is due to the fact already drawn attention to, that there is a pull on a man in two directions in the Nuer kinship system, towards his father's kin and away from them towards his maternal kin, a tension especially marked in the case of an eldest child and in polygamous and concubinary families.

This balance is, as we have seen, very marked in the Nuer kinship system. When one lives among Nuer the relationships of *gwanlen, nar, wac, manlen,* and their children are hardly ever out of one's mind, for there are few conversations in which one or other of them does not figure; and in all discussions of a formal or ceremonial nature they go in pairs of opposites, the paternal uncle with the maternal uncle, the paternal aunt with the maternal aunt, and the sons of the one with the sons of the other. The balance between father's kin and mother's kin is always maintained on important occasions of social life, such as marriages, settlements of feuds, and religious feasts, when relationships are formally defined.

The balance is felt also by Nuer in their everyday life, and it strongly affects the relationships. A mother's brother, for example, is not just a mother's brother. He is, so to speak, a mother's brother and not a father's brother; and the fact that a man has a mother's brother towards whom he can turn in trouble affects his relations with his paternal kin. Relationships are tinged with their opposites. This is not a mere relation of opposites within a formal pattern. We have constantly noted throughout this book the very powerful and frequent attraction of the maternal kin in such a practical question as where a man resides. We have seen that a first-born ought to be brought up by his maternal grandparents; that fatherless young men often go to live with their maternal uncles; that youths frequently stay with their mother's people; that attraction to the maternal kin is accentuated by one or other form of concubinage; and that men easily identify themselves through female links with the lineage with whom they reside. A man has always the choice of several homes, and if he does not care to reside with his paternal kin he can attach himself to the home of other male or female kinsfolk. It is generally towards his mother's brother's people that he turns his eyes when he has disputes with his paternal kin or feels unhappy among them. I had the impression that Nuer, who often talk about it, are very conscious of this pull away from the paternal kin which is personified in the maternal uncle. It signifies not only a balance between paternal and maternal kin within the kinship system but also a balance between the lineage and the society which contains it—between the lineage system and the total social structure.

The relationship between the *gaatnar*, the children of the mother's brother, and the *gaatwac*, the children of the father's sister, who belong to different lineages and, usually, different local communities, is considered by Nuer to be one of easy companionship. Friendship between a man and the sons of his maternal uncle is not blended with the reserve which difference of generation introduces into his relationship with their father. However, the tension personified in the mother's brother cannot but to some extent affect the relationship with his sons. The sons of the mother's brother are the counterpart to the agnatic cousins, the sons of the father's brother, and the two relationships seem for Nuer to stand in opposition.

It remains to say a few words about the *manlen*, the mother's sister. Nuer say of her that she is like the mother's brother, that 'she is your mother', and that she will love you as a son. 'Your mother's sister is your friend. Is she not the sister of your mother?' If you live at her home she will not, like the father's sister, favour her own children at your expense. You are her son and you will eat with her own child and share and share alike with him like brothers. When you visit her from a distance she sees that you are hungry from your journey and at once leaves off what she was doing to prepare a meal for you, and she pours her best butter over the porridge she has prepared for you. It is the mother's sister relationship that Nuer mostly invoke when hurling their spears in hunting and fishing: '*Tet cueda malene*', 'My right hand, my mother's sisters.' This is equal to the *moc*, the invocation of a favourite ox. A mother's sister, like a father's sister, will be asked to contribute a heifer on the marriage of one of her nephews, but she, also, will not be expected to contribute again on the marriage of another son of the same sister. I was told that when a mother's sister dies her nephew may not visit her grave without a goat for sacrifice.

The mother's sister-sister's son relationship belongs to the *gaatnyiet* category, for the children of each of two sisters are children of the daughters of the lineage to the other. Of all Nuer relationships it is the one of the most unadulterated benevolence. The two women and their children may generally be expected to live in different local communities, so that their interrelations are limited to friendly visits. There are none of the elements of opposition which make the relationship of mother's brother to sister's son more complex and explosive. The husbands of the sisters are not likely to be near kinsmen. There are between them none of the bridewealth transactions which complicate the mother's brother-sister's son relationship. There is no pull on the children towards the mother's sister as there is towards the mother's brother and the maternal kinsmen who live in the mother's home. It is perhaps because of the simple affection that the relationship implies to Nuer that *gatmalen*, son of my mother's sister, is a form of address sometimes used to unrelated friends whom a man wishes nevertheless to address by some kinship term.

III

I have been speaking up to the present of relations between close kin, the nuclear kin, who fall in relation to any particular person into a limited number of categories of relationship. These categories make a pattern which we call the kinship system. It was shown in the first chapter how all the members of a person's community are kin (including affines in this term) to him in one way or another, that is, they can all be placed in one or other of these categories. Clearly they are kin in a more remote sense. It is to this more general aspect of the kinship system that I now turn. It is perhaps most conveniently approached in the conventional manner of anthropological writings by an examination of the use of kinship terms.

Nuer kinship terms can be used descriptively to speak of any particular relationship, either with or without reference to a particular person. The construction of these terms is simple, e.g. the father's sister's daughter is *nyawac* (*nya*, daughter, *wac*, father's sister) and the mother's brother's son is *gatnar* (*gat*, son, *nar*, mother's brother). One can combine the primary terms to describe any relationship, e.g. *gatnyawac*, father's sister's daughter's son (*gat*, son, *nya*, daughter, *wac*, father's sister), and *gatgatnar*, mother's brother's son's son (*gat*, son, *gat*, son, *nar*, mother's brother). The terms can, indeed, be presented in a perfectly symmetrical form, for it is correct, though unusual, to say in Nuer *gwanman* (*gwan*, father, *man*, mother) or *gwangwan* (*gwan*, father, *gwan*, father) when speaking of the mother's father or of the father's father if one particularly wishes to distinguish between the maternal and paternal grandfathers; or one can say *demangwan* (*deman*, uterine brother, *gwan*, father) or *gatgwangwan* (*gat*, son, *gwan*, father, *gwan*, father) in speaking of the father's uterine brother or of his paternal half-brother if one wishes to emphasize the distinction, though here again the usage would be cumbersome and uncommon. In fact, it is possible to describe any relationship by combinations of the family terms *gwan*, father, *man*, mother, *deman*, brother, *nyiman*, sister, *gat*, son, and *nya*, daughter, though it would be unusual to describe, for example, the *wac*, father's sister, as *nyimangwan*, sister (daughter of the mother) of the father. Conjugal relationships are very simply indicated by the prefixes *co*, husband, and *ciek*, wife, e.g. *cowac*, husband of the father's sister, and *ciekgatmanlen*, wife of the son of the mother's sister. The husband's affinal relations are denoted by the words for members of the family suffixed by *thu*, e.g. *manthu*, mother-in-law, *nyimanthu*, sister-in-law. The same terms are used for the wife's parents-in-law, but, as we have earlier noted, her husband's brother is her *cocang* and his sister her *mancoa*.

When a Nuer speaks about his family and kin and affines he uses these terms in a slightly different, the possessive, form, e.g. '*gwadong*', 'my grandfather' (paternal and maternal), '*mar*', 'my mother', '*nyimar*', 'my sister', '*gatda*', 'my son', '*wacda*', 'my father's sister', '*nara*', 'my mother's brother', '*gwathu*', 'my wife's (husband's) father', '*conyimar*', 'my sister's husband', &c.

When he addresses them, as in greeting them, he normally uses, and in many cases ought to use, an even simpler nomenclature. Both grandfathers are addressed as '*gwadong*' (or '*gwandong*') and both grandmothers as '*madong*' (or '*mandong*'). The father, his brothers, his paternal cousins, and the husbands of all kinswomen of his and the mother's generation are addressed as '*gwa*', 'father', or sometimes by the respectful form '*gwadin*'; so also are the male kinsmen and affines of the wife by her husband and the male kinsmen and affines of the husband by his wife if they belong to an older generation. A man addresses his mother, his father's other wives, the wives of his father's brothers and paternal cousins, his father's sisters, his mother's sisters, and the wives of all maternal kinsmen of an older generation as '*ma*', 'mother', or sometimes by the respectful form '*madin*', as well as by such terms as '*wacda*', 'my father's sister', and '*malen*', 'my mother's sister'. Also, all those women his wife addresses as '*ma*', 'mother', among her relatives and affines are addressed by the same term by her husband, and all those women the husband calls '*ma*' among his relatives and affines his wife calls '*ma*' also. The maternal uncle is addressed as '*nar*'. A man addresses his brothers and sisters and the sons and daughters of his father's and mother's kinsmen and kinswomen of their generation as '*demar*' (or '*gatmar*'), 'my (uterine) brother', and '*nyimar*', 'my (uterine) sister', as well as by such terms as '*gatwac(da)*', 'son of (my) father's sister', '*nyanar*', 'daughter of (my) mother's brother', and '*gatmalen*', 'son of my mother's sister'. He may likewise address the husbands of kinswomen and the wives of kinsmen as 'brother' and 'sister' if they are of his generation instead of by such terms as '*conyimar*', 'husband of my sister', and '*ciekdemar*', 'wife of my brother'. A man addresses his wife's kinsfolk and affines of her generation and she addresses his kinsfolk and affines of his generation by the same terms. Sons and daughters are addressed as '*gatda*', 'my son', and '*nyada*', 'my daughter', and the sons and daughters of all members of the speaker's paternal and maternal kin of his generation may be addressed by the same terms as well as by '*gatdemar*', 'son of my brother', '*nyademar*', 'daughter of my brother', '*gatnyimar*', 'son of my sister', and '*nyanyimar*', 'daughter of my sister'. The children of affines, and of their affines, of the speaker's generation are also habitually addressed as 'son' and 'daughter', and also their spouses. The children of those addressed as '*gatda*' and '*nyada*' are generally addressed by the same terms, though the son's son may be addressed as '*gatdoda*' and I believe that the daughter's daughter is sometimes addressed as '*nyadoda*'.

In other words, all kinsfolk—paternal, maternal, and affinal—of an ascending generation, except the mother's brother, and even he sometimes, are commonly addressed as '*gwa*', 'father', or '*ma*', 'mother' ('*gwadong*', 'grandfather', and '*madong*', 'grandmother', being only variations meaning 'aged father' and 'aged mother');

all kinsfolk of the speaker's generation are commonly addressed as *'demar'* (or *'gatmar'*), 'my uterine brother', or *'nyimar'*, 'my uterine sister'; and all kinsfolk of the descending generation are commonly addressed as *'gatda'*, 'my son', or *'nyada'*, 'my daughter'.

Even within the family and close kin Nuer use kinship terms so unprecisely that it is only possible to know more or less, when one hears a term used, the type of relationship referred to. A man may be described as *'deman* Cam', 'Cam's uterine brother', when he is in fact his paternal half-brother, or as *'gwan'*, his 'father', when he is in fact his father's brother. A man may describe his relationship to a woman by saying that she is *'nyimar'*, 'my sister', or *'nyama-len'*, 'my mother's sister's daughter'; or he may use both terms, indicating his relationship to her both less and more precisely: *'Nyamemo e nyimar, e nyamalen'*, 'That girl is my sister, is my mother's sister's daughter.' A man may address his maternal uncle as *'nara'*, 'my maternal uncle', or as *'gwa'*, 'father', and the uncle may reply *'gatnyimar'*, 'my sister's son', or *'gatnyieti'*, 'son of daughters', or *'gatda'*, 'my son'. Choice of terms is influenced by the age and genealogical propinquity of the persons concerned. A man may address his *gatnyawac*, the son of his father's sister's daughter, as *'gatnyada'*, 'son of my daughter', and the man may then reply *'gwadong'*, 'my grandfather', but they will also, and usually, address one another as *'demar'*, 'my brother', if they are of about the same age. If a man addresses another of about his age as 'grandfather' he does so jestingly, even though the man in fact stands to him in a classificatory sense in this relationship, e.g. is a member of his maternal grandmother's clan. Although a man may stand to another as maternal uncle in that he is a member of his mother's lineage and of her generation, he is unlikely to address him by the term *'nar'*, 'mother's brother', unless he is closely related to his mother. He is more likely to address him by the general term of respect *'gwa'*, 'father'.

In spite of this vagueness there is discernible in the use by Nuer of their kinship terms a tendency, so general as to be a convention, to place kinsmen in a category of relationship nearer to the speaker than their genealogical relationship to him. As I explained in the last chapter, a man almost invariably uses *'demar'* (or *'gat-mar'*), 'my uterine brother', when speaking to, or about, his pater-nal half-brother instead of *'gatgwar'*, 'my father's son', a term he keeps for the sons of his paternal uncles. He uses *'gatgwalen'*, 'son of my father's brother', for more distant cousins, members of his lineage and clan of his generation. To use *'gatgwalen'* in ordinary conversation for your actual father's brother's son suggests that your relations with him are not cordial. Likewise, to speak to this man's father as *'gwalen'*, 'my father's brother', instead of *'gwa'*, 'father', is suggestive of coldness in the relationship. The same tendency is observable in the use of terms for relatives on the mother's side also. A man calls his mother's sister's son *'gatmar'*, 'son of my mother', and keeps *'gatmalen'*, 'son of my mother's sister', for more distant maternal cousins, or as a courtesy term for unrelated persons. It is bad form to use the correct term for a near kinsman. They say that it is cutting the *gol*, the hearth, off from the *wec*, camp, that is to say, it is drawing a distinction between members of your family and members of the community of kin among whom you live.

Nuer say that when a man uses kinship terms in their exact and literal sense it is because he wishes to stress the precise relationship in which a man stands to him in order to evoke from him some action which is contained in the pattern of behaviour the relationship carries. It generally means that the speaker is asking for a gift or favour: *'Bi e lim ka duob maridun'*, 'You beg for it in the path of your kinship'. Another way of making the same emphasis is by using the *cyot gwan* or *cyot man*, calling the man after the proper name of his father or mother. One also hears the correct usages on ceremonial occasions. One hears them also at dances, for it is then customary for youths to shout them out formally to kinsmen. On such occasions, and as a complimentary usage in chatting, one hears the otherwise rarely used term *'degwar'*, 'son of my father'—the correlative to *'demar'*, 'son of my mother', as *'gatgwar'* is to *'gatmar'*—though it would only be used for paternal cousins and not for the real father's son. I was told that one would also use this term to stress an agnatic link if one required assistance in fighting. The exact usages are also heard when grown-ups or older children are talking to small children about their elders and wish to impress on them the precise relationship in which they stand to them. In like manner, members of the forms of family other than the simple legal family use the same terms of address to one another as members of a simple legal family do, except in such legal or ritual situations as seem to require indication of legal status.

Ordinarily, with near kin relationships are contracted. The

person addressed is taken out of a more distant category of relationship and placed in a more intimate one, but he can be telescoped back again to his genealogical position on occasions. When a Nuer calls a paternal uncle 'father' he is avoiding excluding him from the family circle by calling him 'father's brother'. For this reason terms of relationship are of greater significance among the extra-family kin than they are in the family itself, where intimacy between its members is so self-evident that if any mode of address is required some other mode is commonly employed, such as the use of personal names.

As Nuer have only a limited number of terms of relationship, they have to ring the same changes with them whether a relationship is more or less remote. A paternal cousin six times removed is a *gatgwanlen* no less than a first paternal cousin and can equally be addressed by the terms *'gatgwar'*, 'son of my father', or *'demar'*, 'my uterine brother'. The son of a woman of my mother's clan is *'gatmalen'*, 'my mother's sister's son', whether he is a first cousin or of unknown genealogical distance, and he will equally be addressed as *'gatmar'* or *'demar'*, 'my uterine brother'. Again, any member of the wife's father's or mother's clans is a *gwanthu*, father-in-law, and will therefore be addressed as *'gwa'*, 'father'. Consequently a kinship term, even when used in its right place, can only denote the category of relationship and not its degree. Moreover, the relationship need not be of a direct personal kind at all but may derive from a link between lineages of any distance back. When a man of one lineage has married a woman of another lineage some generations ago all his descendants by her can be regarded, should anyone care to remember the marriage, as *gaat-wac*, children of the paternal aunt, or *gaatnyiet*, children of sisters, by the men of the second lineage, and they can be regarded as *gaatnar*, children of the maternal uncle, by the men of the first. Likewise, lineages descended from sisters can regard each other as *gaatmanlen*, children of the mother's sister. There are so many cross-strands in Nuer society that a man can always find some relationship to another man should he care to do so, and hence place him in one or other of the categories of the kinship system and address him by a term appropriate to this category. Nuer squeeze all members of their communities, all those whom they meet often, into the system somehow. For example, I once asked a Nuer lad why he referred to another man as *'gatgwar'*, 'son of my father', and he replied: 'He is my father's brother's son (*gat-gwalen*)'. As I knew that the two men were either not at all or very distantly related, I asked how this could be. The lad then said that the man was 'a son of my father's distant brother (*gatgwalen ka noni*)'—a distant paternal cousin—and he added: 'He has lived so long among us that I call him "son of my father" ("*gatgwar*"). He has become my father's son. Also, his father and mine were of the same age-set.'

The example I have given introduces a complication, for, quite apart from the kinship system, every adult in Nuer society can be addressed by one of the family relationship terms in virtue of his position in the age-set system. As I have described this system elsewhere it need here be considered only in so far as it is immediately relevant to the subject of kinship. Males are divided into the grades of boys and men, boys being initiated by successive sets into manhood by a severe ordeal. Without discussing the intricacies of the system it may be said that this arrangement of males by age means that from the point of view of any individual man all the other men of his society are formally classed as seniors, equals, and juniors, the division corresponding roughly to three generations —the older, his own, and the younger. To seniors he must show deference, with his equals he is on free and easy terms, and from his juniors he expects deference. Women are brought within the system as being daughters, sisters, and wives of members of sets. The age-set system thus supplements the kinship system in the organization of interpersonal relations in everyday social life. Again without going into details, men of an older generation within the system are 'fathers' and their sisters and wives are 'mothers', men of a man's own generation are 'brothers' ('sons of the father' or 'sons of the mother') and their sisters and wives are 'sisters', and men of a junior generation are his 'sons' and their sisters and wives are his 'daughters'. People address one another accordingly, except that men of the same generation usually salute one another by their ox-names. Thus everybody in Nuerland can be addressed as 'father', 'mother', 'brother', 'sister', 'son', or 'daughter' by reference to their position in the age-set system, and this usage may be regarded as a special instance, and one of the widest radius, of the classificatory use of relationship terms. All men of a man's father's age-set are his 'fathers', and all sons of a man's age-mates are his 'sons', and so forth. A man even speaks collectively of members of a set senior to his own, other than his father's set, as in-laws if they are senior enough for it to be likely that he will marry one of their daughters. In a sense everybody in the age-set system—that is to say, everybody in Nuerland in one way or another—is kin to everybody else, and the word *mar*, kinship, can be used in this connexion: *mar rica*, age-set kin. The use of relationship terms for persons within the system may in part—the common use of personal names may be another reason—account for the very informal, even haphazard, use of kinship terms among the Nuer, for the terminology of address of the age-sets may cut across that of kinship. For example, a man may be to another a classificatory paternal uncle or grandfather genealogically, but if he is of the same generation he is his 'brother' and would so address him and be addressed by him. Contradiction between the two systems is avoided by the assimilation of the values of both to those of the family by the use of the family relationship terms, for though one may not know whether a man is being addressed as 'father' in virtue of his place in the kinship system or in the age-set system, it could never happen that a term appropriate in the one would be inappropriate in the other. It is always correct to address very old persons as 'grandfather' and 'grandmother', persons of one's parents' generation as 'father' and 'mother', persons of one's own generation as 'brother' and 'sister', and persons of the generations of one's children and their children as 'son' and 'daughter'; and this usage may be quite independent of either kinship or age-sets, being merely a courtesy extension of the family terms to all men.

All members of a man's community, whether it be large or small, can thus be addressed by one of the family relationship terms. We do not, I think, understand this convention so well by regarding it, as it is often regarded, as an extension of family terms and sentiments from members of the family to kin as when we regard it as the verbal telescoping of kin into the circle of family reference so that, as Nuer say, the *gol* is not cut off from the *wec*, the hearth from the camp, the family from the community. A man belongs not only to his family but to a wider society.

IV

The classificatory use of terms of relationship is a special problem to be considered separately from the wide recognition of kinship from which it derives. A Nuer, as has been reiterated, establishes a kinship tie with all with whom he has frequent intercourse. Consequently a *ram mo gwagh*, an unrelated person, is a relative term. It signifies a person to whom a man has no genealogical position close enough to prevent intermarriage between their families, someone with whom, even if he could trace relationship, it would be remote. To all intents and purposes he is not kin but a stranger, which amounts to saying that he is neither a close kinsman nor a member of one's immediate local community, that one does not stress a kinship link with him because one has no close social relations with him. Ultimately and potentially everybody is kin, or can be made to appear so if circumstances demand. This is understandable in a society where kinship values are the only guide in interpersonal relations. When a man has constant intercourse with another it is therefore necessary that each be in some category of kinship in respect of the other so that each may have a rough-and-ready guide to the kind of behaviour expected of him and which he may expect from the other. The categories of the kinship system give him only a formal pattern of relationships, and the content of each relationship depends on genealogical distance, proximity of residence, personal feelings, and other factors. But they enable him to systematize his social contacts, to place everybody in a definite position in relation to himself, and so to have the security of living in an ordered world.

Now, as we have noted, these kinship values tend to fall into two broad types, the agnatic type and the type through women. The first is characterized by common group interests and a certain hardness between those who share them, and the second by lack of common group interests and the absence of the jealousies and disharmonies they entail, being no more than a set of separate personal relationships. Relationships of the first type harden into lineage structure, those of the second type remain on an interpersonal kinship footing. This means that a Nuer's contacts with all persons outside the agnatic groups to which he belongs are on a pattern the common design of which is one of tenderness, an attenuated benevolence of family sentiments; and this includes both immediate relationships between persons through female links and, in a lesser degree, relationships between persons through lineage links of the same category at some more or less distant point of time. Thus members of the same lineage are bound to each other by common descent, by ritual ties, by common cattle-interests, by the duty of blood-revenge and other moral obligations, by association with a common territory, and so forth, while they are united within the wider society to persons, and as a group to other lineages, by multiple ties of kinship, all of which lack the ambivalence of agnatic kinship. We have noted, moreover, that the Nuer lineage is not merely a descent group but is a descent group with political functions. It may not therefore be too fanciful to suggest that the agnatic type of kin relationships is associated with the autonomy of political segments and their structural opposition to one another—the process of fission, and the non-agnatic type of kin relationships is associated, through a complex network of ties of this type, with the wider social system which binds these segments together and contains them—the process of fusion. The one set of attitudes emphasizes the singularity and exclusiveness of the agnatic group, in terms of which political values are expressed, and the other emphasizes the community life in which such groups are merged.

In ultimate analysis it might be held that the in-groups, the lineages, and the political units associated with them carry the sentiment of the father-son relationship, and the total community comprised within the multiple strands of the kinship system carries the sentiment of the mother-son relationship. I do not myself hold to such a psychological reduction. I do not think it is true that there are such simple and opposite feelings towards father and mother or that the attitudes to parents are extended to kinsfolk in so simple a manner. I prefer a sociological interpretation in terms of jural relations within the Nuer social system.

I have tried to show in *The Nuer* how the lineage system provides the framework of their political system through the association of lineages with tribal segments, and in this book how, when we examine the constitution of each such segment, we find that it consists of a network of interpersonal kinship ties which connect all its members to one another and directly or indirectly to its dominant lineage, thereby giving to the lineage its corporate character. It is the interaction of the lineage principle with the values of the kinship system which makes any neighbourhood or residential group structurally significant. Through the fusion of all elements into the dominant lineage within each local community, when the community functions as a political unit, the lineage system becomes the organizing principle of the political structure of the wider society which contains it.

The antithesis between kinship and neighbourhood made by Maine and Morgan can therefore be only a logical one and may easily be misleading. Kinship values and political values based on locality are interdependent. All who live together express their relations to one another in terms of the kinship system, and they express their collective interests as a unit in the political system in terms of the lineage system to which they are attached by various kinship ties. The internal network of kinship links gives the local community the cohesion necessary for it to function as a political unity, but it is also true that it is because people are living together that kinship between them is emphasized and effective in the ordering of their interrelations. Hence it is that individuals stress whatever category of kinship is most significant in the particular circumstances of residence in which at any time they find themselves. People do not live together unless they are kin, but kinship is made effective by living together. But though interconsistent, the political system and the kinship system are not only different kinds of system but are on different levels of abstraction. The whole society can be regarded as a network of strands of relationship which regulates relations between persons throughout Nuerland, or can be viewed as a set of relations between local groups in which these strands are ordered by the lineage system into corporate collectivities on the basis of territorial distribution.

In every primitive society we find both family groups and a politically organized society in which they are contained and without which they could not maintain themselves. The values of each affect the other in a two-way movement. The kinship system derives from the family, being, through marriage, built up of a series of families, and it has among the Nuer, as we have seen, an almost limitless extension, at any rate in the sense that everyone can in one way or another and in some degree be placed in a kinship category by everybody else and addressed by them by a kinship term which in common usage is a family relationship term. The whole society is, in this sense, one great family. It has been noted that *mar*, kinship, also means 'my mother', and that this is perhaps significant because all kinship, even with the father and hence with the paternal kin, is through the mother; and in this general sense of kinship one does not grade its categories but gives them equivalence.

The impress of the structural form of the wider society on the kinship system and the family group is no less important. It determines, at any rate to some extent, the emphasis placed on categories of relationship and how far kinship, and therefore descent, are traced through father and mother. It is evident that in Nuer lineages, as I have explained at length in *The Nuer*, agnatic kinship has an extension and depth correlative to their political functions. It may also be suggested that the pull in opposite directions, towards the paternal kin and towards the maternal kin, to which attention has been drawn, is related to the lineage system. The fissiparous tendencies of the lineage system give particular value to the distinction between full brothers and paternal half-brothers in both family and kin, and hence also to the polygamous family and to the position of wives in it. The supremacy of the agnatic principle which the lineage system embodies, also, it has been suggested, by subordinating the roles of the family and of the father to the interests of the wider groups of paternal kin and the lineage, allows the many variants of forms of the family which are so common in Nuerland, and also the widespread adoption of Dinka, the easy translation of affinal and age-set ties into the values of the kinship system, considerable social mobility, and high status of women. All these features seem to be interconsistent.

It may also be suggested that the balance between paternal and maternal kin and in general the equivalence given to all relationships in the kinship system in ordinary social life is related to the lineage system. As we have seen, Nuer lineages are dispersed groups and a man's neighbours belong for the most part to lineages other than his own. Therefore, since Nuer move freely and far, they must trace kinship widely through female links, particularly on the mother's side, as well as agnatically, if they are to make the attachments to persons and lineages which local associations demand, and so live in an ordered world in which every person can be placed in some relationship. The size of a man's local community and the degree of his mobility in it—his social space—affect the manner and range of his counting of kinship, spreading it widely on the mother's side. The individual, it is true, sees the kinship system only in relation to himself and does not reflect on its general social functions, but the student perceives it, without reference to any particular person, as a means by which the members of Nuer society are interconnected in a complex network of numberless strands of relationship. We have noted that the wide tracing of kinship through both father and mother, and indeed through the wife also, and in every direction, is found together, as might be expected, with an extensive distribution of marriage prohibitions, to which the conventions governing bridewealth claims are complementary.

In seeking to understand Nuer society, abstractions from behaviour have been related to one another in order that it may be seen as a whole in the patterns which emerge from the confusion of actualities. We have dealt in this book mainly with the family, the kinship system, and the lineage system, and we have discussed their relations to one another in the whole society, particularly in terms of its political structure to which my earlier book was devoted. As I have explained there, the values of the different social systems operate in different situations and at different levels of social life. I have here attempted to show in demonstration of this thesis how interpersonal kinship relationships deriving from marriage and the family are organized into segments of the political structure through the dominant, or politically significant, lineages which, in the absence of any other principle of organization, alone make possible the large-scale community necessary, in the oecological conditions prevailing, to the Nuer way of life. The dominant lineages have a central position, for at one end they are structural groups with political functions, while at the other end they spread out into relationships of a kinship kind through which the attachments are made which enable them, while remaining distinct descent groups in certain situations, to become in other situations identified with residential groups and so to function politically.

INDEX

Adultery, 41-2. 68, 120-1, 122, 134, 162.
Affines, 6, 9, 12, 16, 19, 20, 23, 24, 26, 33, 35, 78, 86, 89, 143; relations between husband and kin and wife and kin, 59-60, 72, 95-6, 99-104, 134; terms for, 169-70.
Age-sets (ric), 174-5; and kinship, 175; and marriage prohibitions, 33-4, 36, 38, 44, 46; and sacrifices, 154; initiation into, 51, 174; rites of initiation into, 103; use of family terms within system of, 174-5.
Agnates (and agnation), 5, 125, 141, 151, 156-7; and cognation, 16, 17, 19, 157; and descent through mother, 122-3, 156; see also Buth.
Alban, A. H., vi.
Anuak, people, 8, 19, 20, 90.

Balak, a Dinka people, 17.
Beer: at ceremonies, 67; at sacrifice, 154.
Bloodwealth, 98; distribution of, 153.
Bridewealth, 26, 32-3, 34, 40, 49, 53, 60-1, 63, 72, 73, 74-99, 109; and bloodwealth, 98; and marriage rites, 58-9; and sacrifices, 154; circumstances affecting amount of, 82-3; distribution of, 7, 64, 65, 74-89, 153; general functions of, 89-99; payment to genitor of, 31, 87, 88, 108, 116, 121-2; rules regulating return or replacement of, 68 (see also Divorce); some examples of payments today, 87-9; test of nature of union, 121-2; Wangnen cattle of, 77, 80, 81, 143.
Brothers, 77-8; and bridewealth, 75, 76, 81, 159; and ghost-marriage, 111; and levirate, 112-15; and marriage, 79-80, 111, 128, 141, 143; distinction between full and half-brothers, 79-80, 114, 127, 135, 141-5, 154, 163; paternal half-brothers and bridewealth, 75, 76, 81; uterine, 37, 45-6, 145, 161; wives of, 78, 97, 103, 130.
'Bull' (tut): agnatic category, 145, 156, 166; and incest, 37-8, 39, 41, 45; man holding leading position in local community, 9, 16, 22, 27-8; woman as, 17-18.
Buor (mud windscreen), 65, 104, 127.
Burridge, K. O. L., vii.
Buth (agnatic kinship between lineages), 6-7, 25, 34, 154; see also Agnates.

Cattle, 27, 89; see also Bridewealth.

Cattle camps, 2, 3-4, 125; see also Wec.
Children: and bridewealth, 84-5; and parents, 136-8; and sex, 50-1; born 'in the bush', 91-3, 115, 117; born into circle of kin, 135; called after genitor, 150; called after one or other parent, 12; complete marriage, 71-3, 74, 108; eldest (keagh), 27, 72-3, 136, 139; make kinship between parents, 33, 43, 45, 96, 103-4, 139; taught relationships, 172; youngest (pek), 139.
Cieng (home, community, &c.), 1, 3, 5, 12, 18, 21, 23, 24, 38.
Concubines, 106-7; and incest, 43; and marriage prohibitions, 36; unmarried (keagh), 17, 21, 26, 98, 117-20; widow-, see under Widows.
Coriat, P., vi.
Courtship, 38-9, 49-58, 70.
Crazzolara, Father J. P., vi.

Dances, 1-2, 51-4, 60, 62, 65, 68, 155, 172.
Daughters: terminus of family, 109, 125, 145.
Dep (war or dancing line of a village), 2, 52, 54, 62.
Dhor (hamlet), 3.
Dil (tribal aristocrat), 9.
Dinka (Jang), 19, 151, 160; adoption of, 7, 8, 19, 20, 23, 24-5, 32, 36; as lover, 22, 108, 112; descent, 19, 20; effects of absorption of, 20; marriage with, 20, 32; of various origins, 20; women captives, 133, 134.
Divorce, 70, 91-6, 113, 114, 115; reasons for, 134; see also Bridewealth.

Exogamy, 6, 20, 30, 36, 44, 47.

Family, 3, 4; and community, 172, 175, 178; and kinship and lineage, 122-3, 131, 151, 172, 178-9; an economic unit, 129-32; elementary, 127; forms of, 104-23, 145-51; ghost-, 110, 129, 146-7; leviratic, 113, 129, 147-8; modes of address in, 173; natural, 116-17, 119-20, 148-51; polygamous, 108, 127, 140; relations within, 132-51; simple legal, 108, Chap. IV, 146; terms, classificatory use of, 170-1, 175.
Father (gwan): and bridewealth, 75, 80; curse of, 138; position of, in family, 124; sacrifice in honour of dead, 154; see also Pater and Genitor.

(181)

INDEX

Father's brother (*gwanlen*), 23, 144, 153, 157–9; and bridewealth, 64, 75, 80, 158–9, 161; and wedding, 67; children of (*gaatgwanlen*), 24, 113, 157, 159–60.

Father's sister (*wac*), 24, 106, 107, 160–1; and bridewealth, 75, 81, 128, 153, 161; children of (*gaatwac*), 5, 16, 106, 167.

Feuds, 6.

Food: and affines, 99, 101, 102; and opposite sex, 51, 55; and spouses, 102; shared among kin, 132; and family relations, 135, 158.

Gaatbol, clan, 16.

Gaatnyiet (children of daughters), category of kinship through women, 16, 23, 145, 157, 161, 165–6, 168, 176–7.

Genitor, 18, 31, 120–1, 150; *see also* Bridewealth *and* Family, natural.

Ghosts, 60, 62, 66, 70, 81, 91, 104, 109–12, 125, 129, 155, 163.

God (*Gwandong*), 66.

Gol (hearth, family, home, &c.), 3, 4, 5, 32, 49, 125, 127, 152, 172, 175.

Gordon, Bimb. H., 91.

Gwagh (unrelated), 39; a relative term, 176.

Gwan buthni (master of ceremonies), 62, 64–6, 70, 71, 86, 125.

Hide, cow of the, 41, 121.

Homestead, 3, 124–7.

Howell, P. P., vi, 91, 121.

Incest (*rual*), Chap. II.

Jackson, H. C., 91.

Jang (Dinka), 21; *see under* Dinka.

Jidiet, clan, 21.

Jikany, tribe, 7, 54.

Jikul, clan, 25.

Jimem, clan, 20, 21, 25.

Jinaca (Gaatnaca), clan, 9, 21, 22, 36.

Joking-relationship, 159–60.

Keagh (unmarried mother or unmarried concubine), 53; *see also* Concubines, unmarried.

Kiek, clan, 22, 25.

Kiggen, Father J., vi, 103.

Kingdon, F. D., vi.

Kinship (*mar*), Chap. IV; affines regarded as kin, 6, 12, 96, 100–1, 104, 156; and age-sets, 174–5; and ceremonies, 71; and Dinka, 20, 25; and family, 130–2, 152, 154–5, 172; and gifts, 132; and lineage, 4–8, 20, 179–80; and neighbourhood, 178; and political system, 178–80; and ven-

geance, 155; and village and camps, Chap. I; balance between maternal and paternal kin, 6, 35, 74, 151, 152–3, 166; categories of, 152–4, 156–68, 173; close, or nuclear, kin, 154–5, 156; complications due to ghost-marriage, 111–12; distribution of bridewealth, bloodwealth, &c., among categories of, 153–4; features of paternal, 162, 176–7; formal breaking of, 31, 35; importance of maternal ties of, 19, 21, 107, 115–16, 143, 144, 148; in intercommunity fighting, 155; maternal link treated as paternal one, 16, 17, 19, 23, 151; natural, 21–2, 25–6, 31, 86, 150; network of ties of, v, 24, 27, 29, 47, 58, 173, 178; obligations of, 109, 154–5; other meanings of the word *mar*, 156; paternal kin defined, 7; pull in two directions by, 140, 151, 166–7; radius of effective, 4; severing of (*dakene mar*), 80, 138, 153, 155; swearing (*kwith*) among kin, 155; terms, 7, 132, 135, 142, 156, 165, 168–75; wide recognition of, 8, 29, 156, 176; wider aspects of, 168–80; *see also* Incest.

Konye, village, 8–12.

Kurmayom, village, 12, 21–2.

Labour: division of, 129–30; co-operation in, 131–2.

Leek, tribe, 12, 16.

Leopard-skin chief, 42, 64.

Lewis, B. A., vi.

Lienhardt, R. G., vii.

Lineage: and byre, 125; and marriage, 97–8, 122–3; and paternal kin, 162; and polygamous family, 140–1, 144; and the wider society, 140, 167; and tribal structure, v, 20–1, 23, 177–8; an exclusive descent group, 6, 23; a residential group, 3, 17; attachments to, 17, 18, 19, 20, 22, 23; core of local communities, 16, 19, 23; difference between kinship and, 4–8, 23–4, 47; dominant in tribe, 15, 18, 19; kinship links between lineages, 5, 173; political functions of, 1, 5, 46–7, 180; social identification with villages of, 2, 16; stability of structure of, 28, 151; *see also Thok dwiel* and *thok mac* (lineage).

Lou, tribe, 7, 8, 9, 17, 21, 54.

Maine, Sir Henry, 178.

Mancom, village, 105–7.

Marriage, 49; age at which sexes marry, 57, 61; ceremonies, 58–73;

PRINTED IN GREAT BRITAIN
AT THE UNIVERSITY PRESS, OXFORD
BY VIVIAN RIDLER
PRINTER TO THE UNIVERSITY